1000 World War 2 Facts

Tom Chapman

Introduction

Think you know all there is to know about World War 2? Well, think again. 1000 World War 2 Facts contains all the fascinating trivia you could ever wish to know about the theatres of war, the Axis, the Allies, weapons, battles, atrocities, the Nazis, Hitler, ships, aircraft, submarines, and much more.

(1) When the German Sixth Army became trapped in Stalingrad their rations quickly dwindled because it became impossible for the Luftwaffe (the German air force) to drop sufficient supplies. The Soviets erected field kitchens around the encircled area so that the starving Germans would have to endure the sensual torture created by the aroma of hot food.

(2) In the last weeks of the war, a German theology student named Robert Limpert tried to save his home town of Anbasch from needless destruction. Limpert distributed leaflets calling for a peaceful surrender to the Americans. The student was hanged in public after being reported by some Hitler Youth children.

(3) Adolf Hitler's nephew William Hitler (later William Stuart-Houston) served in the US Navy during the war. William was born to Adolf Hitler's half-brother Alois Hitler Jr in Liverpool, England. He later emigrated to the United States and joined the navy - where he won a Purple Heart after being wounded in action.

(4) Three million people were trapped in the siege of Leningrad. The German Army surrounded the Soviet city and enforced a blockade designed to starve the inhabitants to death. People got so hungry they even ate wallpaper. By the end of the siege, 260 Leningraders had been arrested for cannibalism.

(5) Superman comics qualified as essential supplies for the US Marine garrisons at Midway Islands during World War 2.

(6) During their invasion of the Soviet Union, the German soldiers would sometimes find themselves fighting in snow over a metre deep in a temperature of minus 30 degrees.

(7) When British soldiers liberated Bergen-Belsen concentration camp, they discovered some lampshades that had been made from human skin.

(8) In March 1945, American bombers dropped 1,665 tons of bombs on Tokyo. Sixteen square miles of the city was flattened and destroyed.

(9) In December, 1941, soldiers of the Das Reich SS Division reached the terminus of the Moscow city tramcar system. This was the farthest any German soldier ever reached in the drive on Moscow. Two days later, the Red Army began a winter offensive and Das Reich had to retreat.

(10) A soldier captured by the Americans during the invasion of Normandy was initially thought to be Japanese but he was actually a Korean named Yang Kyoungjong who in 1938 had been forced to fight for the Japanese Kwantung Army in Manchuria. He was then captured by the Red Army during the battle of Khalkhin Gol in 1939 and forced to fight for the Soviet Union after spending time in a labour camp. In 1943, Kyoungjong was captured by the Germans during the Battle of Kharkov in Ukraine and ended up in the Atlantic Wall near 'Utah Beach' as a German conscript where his incredible war finally came to an end with D-Day.

(11) The Japanese military practised cannibalism near the end of World War 2. The Allied authorities knew of this but suppressed the details when the war ended for fear of upsetting relatives of lost soldiers.

(12) Adolf Hitler once controlled more territory than the Holy Roman Empire. There was a point in the war where Hitler had almost the whole European land mass and large parts of the Soviet Union and North Africa under German domination.

(13) Foo fighters was the name given to mysterious aerial phenomena reported by Allied pilots in Europe. They consisted of white spheres of light that appeared to follow the aircraft. These objects could not be shot down and did not show up on radar. There is naturally a theory that they might have been some sort of experimental Nazi wonder weapon. More mundane explanations are St Elmo's Fire, ice crystals, or

flak.

(14) 80% of all German military loses in World War 2 happened on the eastern front in the war against the Soviet Union.

(15) Believe it or not, the Soviets deployed some old-fashioned cavalry divisions against the Germans. Soldiers on Siberian ponies wielding sabres would raid German camps at night.

(16) A Japanese soldier named Hiroo Onoda was discovered on the Pacific island of Lubang in 1974. He had been living in the jungle for nearly thirty years and didn't know that the war had ended.

(17) Adolf Hitler appointed himself as the supreme commander of the German armed forces. Many German generals secretly regarded this to be laughable because Hitler had never risen above the rank of corporal in his own military career.

(18) The author Graeme Donald claimed in a book that the Nazis had a scheme in 1940 to supply soldiers with Aryan blow up dolls in order to prevent their troops from picking up sexually transmitted diseases from prostitutes. Donald said that Hitler and Heinrich Himmler (the head of the SS) approved the plan but the plug was pulled in 1942 because soldiers didn't like the dolls. Donald's book also claimed that Hungarian actress Kathe von Nagy refused a request to have her likeness on the doll.

(19) The Italian dictator Mussolini suffered from a stomach ulcer and had an eccentric diet. He only ate rice, eggs, boiled onions, a small amount of meat, and a lot of fruit. One visitor said Mussolini ate 7 pounds of grapes a day and only drank milk.

(20) The Nazis developed jet fighters (most famously the German Me-262) before the end of World War 2 but there

were too few of these planes and insufficient fuel and pilots to make any difference to the outcome of the conflict. There was also unhelpful confusion and debate over whether the planes should be used as a fighter or bomber.

(21) Near the end of the war, the Allies were concerned that the Nazis were going to make a last stand in an Alpine Fortress (Alpenfestung) where they had built impregnable fortifications and had underground stores of munitions. The Germans never activated any such plan though. The Alpenfestung was mostly propaganda spun by Göbbels to stir Allied paranoia. The aim of Göbbels was to make Germany seem stronger than it actually was.

(22) On the eastern front, Soviet aircraft would drop incendiary bombs on huts and farmhouses so that German soldiers had nowhere to get out of the cold.

(23) Nazi Germany (and its territories) was administered by the Gauleiters - who each had their own region to govern. They were ardent Nazis and Hitler loyalists who ruled with ruthless brutality. When the war turned sour for Germany, the Gauleiters were usually the most vociferous in demanding that soldiers fight to the last man or be executed and that civilians must not flee. When it came to practicing what they preached, the Gauleiters were no example to anyone, secretly fleeing themselves the first chance they got with their looted art treasures and leaving woman and children to fend for themselves.

(24) Barbarossa was the codename for the invasion of the Soviet Union by Nazi Germany on the 22nd of June 1941. Barbarossa or Red Beard was a term for Emperor Frederick I. Three million German soldiers were involved in the initial invasion and although it began with great success, the industrial and manpower resources of the Soviet Union were eventually too vast for the Germans to overcome. The decision to invade the Soviet Union is regarded by most historians to be the biggest mistake Hitler made during the war.

(25) The Battle of Britain began on July the 10th 1940. Nazi Germany could only invade Great Britain by sea and land if they first had control of the skies. This task fell to the Luftwaffe but they never managed to achieve this thanks to the dogged resistance put up by the pilots of the Royal Air Force. Hitler soon abandoned plans to invade Britain and decided to concentrate on the invasion of the Soviet Union. The bravery of the British and Allied pilots in the Battle of Britain led to one of Winston Churchill's most famous quotes - Never in the field of human conflict have so many owed so much to so few.

(26) In the early years of the war, the Nazis used the Reserve Police Battalion to murder Jews. The battalion killed an estimated 80,000 Jewish people. Although it was made up of ordinary German people from a cross section of society, only 2% of the battalion's members refused to take part in the mass shootings. 98% of the members were perfectly happy to spend their day shooting innocent Jewish people.

(27) D-Day was the name given to the Allied invasion of Nazi controlled continental Europe in World War 2. It was launched on June the 6th 1944 from England. The invasion was called Operation Overlord and targeted an 80km area of the Normandy coast in France. D-day is the largest invasion by sea in history.

(28) At the start of Operation Barbarossa, the Soviets lost 2,000 aircraft in two days.

(29) Hitler's distinctive toothbrush mustache is alleged to have originated from his service in the First World War. It is speculated that Hitler had to trim his (more traditional) mustache to wear a gas mask.

(30) Hamburgers in America were called Liberty Steaks during World War 2 so they would sound less German.

(31) Over one million children died in the Holocaust.

(32) 40,000 men served on Nazi U-boats during the war. Only 10,000 survived.

(33) Adolf Hitler correctly predicted that the Allies would land in Normandy. However, he then changed his mind and said the Allies would land in Calais. As a consequence of this, the German 15th Army was stationed at Calais on D-Day waiting for a landing that never arrived.

(34) Despite peddling fanatical nonsense about the 'master race', the leading Nazis were a bizarre and sickly bunch. Hitler was beset with medical ailments, Goebbels was short with a club foot, and Himmler was a disconcertingly odd looking man with bad eyesight.

(35) The Maginot Line was a series of fortifications built by the French in the 1930s to protect themselves from any German aggression. It was manned by the French army and even had its own subway system. It proved to be ineffective in World War 2 because the Germans aimed the focal point of their attack at the Ardennes region of Belgium and simply bypassed the Maginot Line.

(36) 70,000 French civilians were killed by Allied offensive action during the course of the war. This is greater than the number of British people killed by German air raids.

(37) The Battle of the Bulge is also known as the Ardennes Offensive. This was the last major German offensive of World War 2 and took place close to Christmas in 1944. The ambitious aim of the offensive was to capture the port of Antwerp in Belgium and split the American and British forces. Hitler believed that the Allies would lose their appetite for war as a consequence of the Ardennes Offensive and it would then allow him to transfer men and tanks to the east where they were badly needed to fight the Soviet Union. But with the Germans lacking experienced battle hardened soldiers and desperately short of fuel for tanks and vehicles, the offensive

quickly petered out and fell hopelessly short of expectations. All it did was shorten the war because German armies in the west were now even weaker after the losses in men and tanks.

(38) On the 16th of April, 1945, the Red Army attacked (General Heinrici's) Army Group Vistula. Army Group Vistula was the only thing standing between the Soviets and Berlin. As part of the attack, the Red Army deployed 143 gigantic searchlights. The idea was to blind and terrify the German defenders and make night seem like day. As it turned out, the lights did more to dazzle and discombobulate the Soviet attackers than the German defenders.

(39) A twelve year-old boy named Calvin Graham lied about his age during the war and served in the US Navy. His deception was only uncovered when he got injured.

(40) Nearly 20,000 French civilians were killed during the Allied invasion of Normandy.

(41) The Germans never seized the vital British colony of Gibraltar in the Mediterranean because of an impasse between (Spanish dictator) Franco and Hitler. Franco believed Spanish forces should have this mission but Hitler thought German forces should stage the operation. As a consequence, Hitler refused to supply any weapons, aircraft, or naval support for a Spanish attack on Gibraltar. This was secretly a relief to Franco. Franco was very reluctant to get involved in the war because he knew the British (who had a large navy) could blockade Spain if they wanted to. Britain was also secretly giving Spain money to stay neutral. Britain nonetheless evacuated 16,000 people from Gibraltar in case of any attempt to seize the rock.

(42) 85% of German soldiers in Soviet prisoner of war camps died in captivity.

(43) The United States built 48,000 aircraft and 25,000 tanks in 1942. This was considerably more than Nazi Germany could

manage. The industrial might of the United States gave the Allies a huge material advantage over Germany.

(44) In 1935, Marshall Tukhachevskii, the first Deputy Commissar for Defence, staged a simulated 'war game' to test how the Soviet Union would fare in the event of an invasion by Nazi Germany. The conclusion was that the Red Army's dispositions and active strength would make it very vulnerable to a surprise German attack of considerable weight. Stalin was so irritated by this report that Tukhachevskii was murdered along with most of the officer corps in a merciless purge.

(45) The Coca-Cola Company set up bottling plants in North Africa during the war so that American soldiers in Europe always had coke to drink.

(46) Operation Barbarossa went so well at first that Hitler even began talking about a victory parade in Moscow.

(47) French SS troops offered the last resistance to the Red Army before they reached Hitler's bunker.

(48) Adolf Hitler's favourite general was Walther Model. Model became known as the Führer's Fireman because he was always sent in to tidy up a situation which appeared hopeless or precarious. Model was a staunch Nazi and stern disciplinarian (two qualities that obviously made him popular with Hitler).

(49) Over 100,000 Allied bomber crewmen were killed in Europe during the war.

(50) By the end of 1941, Moscow was under threat and the Germans controlled over half of the grain, coal and steel available to the Soviet Union. Around seven million Red army soldiers had been killed or captured. 18,000 tanks and 14,000 aircraft had been destroyed by the Germans. The Germans (wrongly) assumed that the Soviet Union was finished.

(51) 3,000 British, American, and Canadian troops died on D-Day.

(52) Pearl Harbour was attacked by 350 Japanese fighter planes, bombers, and torpedo planes in two waves on the 7th of December 1941. Three cruisers, three destroyers, a minelayer, and 188 aircraft were destroyed in the attack and 2,403 Americans were killed. The Japanese had gambled that a surprise attack on Pearl Harbour would destroy the US Pacific Fleet and render the Americans unable to wage war with them. However, six of the eight American battleships that got hit were refloated and repaired and the aircraft carriers stationed at Pearl Harbour were at sea at the time of the attack and so suffered no damage whatsoever. The damage to the US Pacific Fleet was nowhere near as catastrophic as it could have been.

(53) Albert Speer was an architect who Hitler became fond of and made Minister of Armaments. Near the end of the war, Hitler ordered a scorched earth policy where Germany's industrial infrastructure was to be destroyed. He wanted to go down in a blaze of destruction. Speer knew this would be a crime against the German people and cause needless suffering after the war so he did his best to secretly block these orders where he could.

(54) Albert Speer was sentenced to 20 years in prison after the war. Upon his release, he wrote books and appeared on TV shows. He cast himself as the 'decent' Nazi who had tried to end the suffering and even plotted to kill Hitler. It was true that he had tried to stop the destruction of German industry but Speer had also ruthlessly exploited slave labour to keep the German munitions industry going and done as much as anyone to needlessly prolong the war. Documents have also proved that Speer, who was part of Hitler's inner circle, knew of the concentration camps and mass genocide.

(55) In 1939 the United States had 29 shipyards building ships for the navy. By 1942 this number had increased to 322.

(56) During the entire conflict, Germany never had less than 60% of its soldiers on the eastern front.

(57) When it comes to statistics, Stalin was an even more prolific mass murderer than Hitler. Stalin sent millions to their deaths in labour camps (Gulags).

(58) Operation Sea Lion was the codename for the Nazi invasion of Britain. This invasion never took place because the Luftwaffe could not secure control of British airspace. The Germans planned to land 25 army divisions on the south coast of England.

(59) While fighting on the eastern front, the 3rd SS Panzer Division became stranded and had to survive in the snowbound Demyansk Pocket for 73 days until it was relieved. The division consisted of around 20,000 men but only 6,000 were left when it was relieved.

(60) General Patton was one of the first American generals to feature in the German High Command War Diary. The Germans noted that Patton's army was very tenacious and always on the offensive. Patton reminded them of their own great Panzer generals from the early days of the war.

(61) Stalin would never visit the front and always stayed in Moscow (even when it appeared to be in danger of attack). His generals always felt his presence though - however far away he was. Stalin was always on the telephone to them and would dispatch some very sardonic and blunt telegrams to any general he felt was not performing as he should do.

(62) The Red Army began using the Katyusha rocket system on the battlefield in 1941. This could fire over 300 rockets in 20 seconds.

(63) When the Allies invaded on D-Day, German generals and officers could only move formations or give new strategic

orders if Hitler consented. One general said he telephoned Berlin during the battle to ask consent to move a formation but was told Hitler was asleep and that he should call back later.

(64) Operation Bagration was a Red Army offensive launched in June 1944. The offensive was aimed at German forces in the Byelorussian Soviet Socialist Republic and Poland. The offensive destroyed the 50 divisions of Germany's Army Group Centre. Over half a million German soldiers were killed or captured and a seven hundred mile gap in the German front was opened. Operation Bagration was the largest and most devastating offensive of the entire war.

(65) Late in the war, Hitler created a new formation called Army Group Vistula. It was the last scrapings from the bottom of the barrel. Hitler appointed Heinrich Himmler - a man with no military experience whatsoever - as the commander of the newly formed Army Group Vistula. Himmler set up his HQ in a luxury train and soon proved to be completely out of his depth. He cluelessly built an east-west defence line from the Vistula to the Oder which merely served as protection from Pomerania in the north. Himmler was barricading the side entrance and leaving the front door wide open.

(66) The United States produced 325,000 aircraft during the war.

(67) Stalin was tiny in real life. He was only 5'4.

(68) Even in the last weeks and months of the war, an unquantifiable number of Germans somehow managed to maintain some faith in Hitler and the military situation because of the so called wonder weapons. People knew of the V rockets and jet-fighters and wrongly assumed that Hitler had something even more amazing up his sleeve that he was waiting to unleash at the last minute. These mythical wonder weapons maintained some hope as the war came ever closer to home.

(69) In the last days of the Battle of Stalingrad, Hitler made the trapped Sixth Army's commander Colonel General Friedrich von Paulus a Field Marshal. The subtext of this move was obvious. No German officer of that rank had ever been captured alive and so Hitler was reminding von Paulus of his duty to commit suicide. Hitler was furious when he found out that von Paulus had surrendered and had no intention of killing himself.

(70) The German army was shocked by the cold weather in the Soviet Union when the winter came. Their automatic weapons froze and their hot soup ration would be freezing and have ice crystals by the time it was served.

(71) The most important (in terms of their proximity to Hitler) German staff officers in the war were Generalfeldmarschall Wilhelm Keitel (OKW, Supreme Command of the German Armed Forces) and Generaloberst Alfred Jodl (Chief of the Operations Staff of OKW). These men owed their position though to the fact that they never stood up to Hitler and simply agreed with anything he proposed. The other German generals considered Keitel and Jodl to be yes men and lackeys. Neither was taken seriously at all as a strategist or independent military thinker.

(72) Roosevelt really disliked General de Gaulle. He could barely stand to be in the same room.

(73) Khalkhin Gol was a skirmish in 1939 on the Mongolian frontier between the Japanese and Soviets. The Japanese came off second best in the encounter. It is speculated that the experience of this made Japan abandon their plans to invade Siberia.

(74) Britain supplied three-quarters of the ships and two-thirds of the aircraft for D-Day.

(75) By the end of the war, the American defence budget was

fifty times larger than it had been at the start of the war.

(76) The two main Axis powers Germany and Japan acted independently of each other and in a sense got Stalin off the hook. It was only because of Japan's disinterest after Khalkhin Gol that Stalin was able to use his Far East divisions to help save Moscow and Stalingrad. If Japan had attacked the Soviet Union from the east when Stalin's forces were in their darkest hours fighting the Germans then it's hard to see how the Red Army could have regained its equilibrium.

(77) General Patton famously had to apologise to his entire army when he slapped a recuperating soldier in Sicily.

(78) During the war, a fifth of the population of Britain believed in the paranormal. Believe it or not, some witches threw a substance known as 'go-away' powder into the sea to deter Nazi invaders.

(79) During their invasion of the Soviet Union, the Germans fought alongside Italian and Romanian satellite armies. The Italian and Romanian soldiers on the eastern front were what you might call reluctant allies. They had antiquated equipment and no great appetite for battle. The Soviets often targeted the areas held by the Italian and Romanian divisions because these formations were much weaker than the German divisions.

(80) Most historians think that the best British general of the war was William Slim. Slim was the commander of the Fourteenth Army in Burma. The Fourteenth Army became known as the Forgotten Army because they received little publicity compared to armies fighting in Europe and Africa.

(81) Japanese soldiers sometimes used bicycles to move through the jungle more quickly.

(82) The Germans lost over 100,000 men in the Battle of the Bulge.

(83) The United States built 88,000 tanks during the war. This was surpassed by the Soviet Union - who built 105,000 tanks. Nazi Germany built 46,000 tanks so one can see how dwarfed they were by the military and industrial might of their enemies.

(84) Believe it or not, Hitler was actually surprisingly popular in Germany even up to 1944 (when by that stage it was obvious that Germany had lost the war). When the attempt was made on Hitler's life by Claus von Stauffenberg and disgruntled army officers, many people in Germany were shocked and appalled by what they saw as an act of gross treason.

(85) What saved the Soviet Union as much as anything from defeat against Nazi Germany was the sheer size of the country. There were always vast amounts of territory to withdraw to and use to build new munitions factories. The length of the front the Germans had to hold became unsustainable.

(86) When it came to tanks and heavy weapons, the Germans were often more advanced than the Allies. However, the Germans could not replace losses in men and equipment in the same way that the Allies could. The Allies also ruled the skies - a vital factor in any battle.

(87) Nazi U-boats sank 2000 Allied ships.

(88) Germany executed over 20,000 of its own soldiers for cowardice or desertion during the war. In the whole of the war, Britain executed 40 of its soldiers.

(89) Stalin enforced discipline within his armies and population with special NKVD squads. This ruthless organisation was used to keep reluctant soldiers and workers obedient during battles - a bullet the main instrument of persuasion.

(90) The Battle of Midway was a pivotal naval duel fought in

June 1942. The US Navy lost a carrier and a destroyer but the Japanese lost four aircraft carriers and a heavy cruiser. The loss of four aircraft carriers and 250 aircraft was a devastating blow to the Japanese and titled the tide in the Pacific war.

(91) The Winter War of 1939/40 took place when the Soviet Union invaded Finland. The Red Army suffered a bloody nose in this conflict despite their huge material advantages. The Winter War was one of the reasons why Hitler had a low opinion of the Red Army.

(92) Of 110,000 German soldiers captured at Stalingrad, only 5,000 ever returned home.

(93) Some biographers (and even a few people who cooked for Hitler) have said it is a myth that he was vegetarian. The theory is that Hitler's vegetarianism was a myth invented by Joseph Goebbels to make Hitler seem ascetic and abstemious.

(94) The Heinkel He-111, the Luftwaffe's twin-engine bomber, was originally conceived as a passenger aircraft.

(95) In the later stages of the war, a solitary artillery attack by the Soviets in the east killed a quarter of the German 4th Army in one engagement.

(96) A big factor in the early success of the German advance in the Battle of the Bulge was foggy weather. This meant the Allied planes were temporarily grounded.

(97) When he was an impoverished artist as a young man, Hitler briefly lived in a homeless shelter.

(98) The Volkssturm (People's Storm) was a militia organisation created by Goebbels in the last months of the war. The Volkssturm was made up of men who would have previously been considered too old or too unfit to be in the army. Goebbels wanted the Volkssturm to provide millions of men to fight tenaciously alongside the German Army. Despite

his grand plans and dreams, the Volkssturm proved to be completely useless. The recruits in the Volkssturm lacked sufficient weapons and training and were often pushed into battle with not much more than an armband. Many members of the Volkssturm simply fled and those that did fight were little more than cannon fodder.

(99) Near the end of the war it took 290 trains to move the 6th SS Panzer Army from the west to Hungary.

(100) Hitler told General Gerd von Rundstedt that the war against the Soviet Union would last ten weeks.

(101) According to the book Invisible Eagle, in 1942 the Nazis used a Baltic Island to keep their radar sets at a specific angle for several days in order to prove that the earth is not a sphere floating in space but a bubble set in an infinity of rock.

(102) In the last stages of the war, when Germany desperately needed more manpower for the army and the munitions factories, Hitler refused a request to transfer workers in confectionery factories to more vital occupations because he thought it would be bad for morale if people couldn't buy chocolate and sweets.

(103) Gordon Frederick Cummins was a killer who became known as The Blackout Ripper for murdering four women during the German bombing raids on London in World War 2. Cummins, who was in the Royal Air Force, was a very sick and savage killer. He slashed one woman's throat with a can opener and would sexually mutilate the victims. Cummins was hanged in Wandsworth Prison in 1942.

(104) An abandoned German plan early in the war proposed that three entire German Army Groups should be used to capture Gibraltar, Tripolitania and the Suez Canal.

(105) In the last weeks of the war, General Walther Wenck's Twelfth Army and a rag-tag collection of units commanded by

General Felix Steiner were ordered by Hitler to attack at two separate points against the Red Army and relieve Berlin. In reality, Wenck's Army had been defeated weeks ago and Steiner's forces were so weak he never even forwarded Hitler's preposterous orders to his officers. When Hitler heard that his order to attack had been ignored he launched a furious tirade. Thanks to the film Downfall, this tirade is now an internet meme.

(106) General Schlemm, commander of the First German Parachute Army, said it was obvious by July 1944 that Germany couldn't win the war.

(107) The British defence of Singapore and Burma in the early years of the war was something of a fiasco. Some of this (especially Singapore) was partly because of poor leadership but the another problem was that Winston Churchill had made the Middle East the priority for tanks and aircraft. This was done at the expense of the Far East.

(108) While other Nazis were always going off to Tibet to search for ancient races and secrets or consulting the stars, Hitler never had much time for it himself beyond the symbolism.

(109) In the last months of the war, Nazi Germany found itself completely alone. Italy was knocked out of the war, the Romanians and Bulgarians switched sides, and Finland ended its alliance with Germany. Even the Japanese suggested that Hitler should start armistice negotiations with Stalin or the Allies.

(110) Many Japanese soldier corpses in the Mariana Islands were found to be missing the heads. This was because American soldiers were collecting skulls.

(111) The Americans wanted to invade Europe in 1942 and generally saw North Africa and the Mediterranean campaigns as sideshows. They wanted to take the quickest and most

direct approach possible to defeating Nazi Germany. The British thought that invading Europe too soon (while Germany was still strong) would be a mistake.

(112) 400,000 Germans, 200,000 Romanians, 130,000 Italians, and 120,000 Hungarians were killed, wounded or captured in the battle for Stalingrad.

(113) After fourteen days in Normandy, the American, British and Canadian casualties came to 5,287 killed, 23,079 wounded and 12,183 missing.

(114) Heinrich Muller was one of the most wanted Nazis to evade the Allied authorities. Muller was head of the Gestapo and last seen in the Hitler's bunker in the last days of the war. It is believed he must have died attempting to escape from Berlin.

(115) 1,200 warships were involved in D-Day.

(116) The United States spent $350 billion on the war. This was more than Britain and the Soviet Union spent combined.

(117) The first Nazi concentration camp was established in Germany in 1933.

(118) Most of the boots worn by the Red Army in World War 2 were supplied by the United States.

(119) Around 5,000 people in Britain were killed by V-1 rockets with many more injured. The rockets were not impossible to shoot down though and didn't have the devastating impact that Hitler had hoped for.

(120) Over 3,000 V-2 rockets were fired by Germany. The main target was Britain but Antwerp was also targeted as the Germans retreated.

(121) The V-2 rockets made no significant impact on the war

and were incredibly expensive. German propaganda pretended that the V-2 was devastating Britain and destroying British morale but this wasn't really the case.

(122) The Germans had plans to launch V-2 rockets at the United States from U-boat decks but nothing came of this.

(123) Like the Nazi jet fighter bomber, the V-2 rocket came on stream too late in the war to have any great significance.

(124) One of Hitler's favourite generals was Ferdinand Schörner - who he made a Field Marshal. Schörner was a staunch Nazi and notoriously brutal. Schörner had more men shot for cowardice and alleged desertion than any other general. However, like many Nazis, Schörner did not practice what he preached. Near the end of the war, Schörner abandoned his army command and secretly flew west in civilian clothes in an attempt to surrender to the Americans rather than the Soviets.

(125) Schörner's Army Group Centre (which was fighting the Red Army in Czechoslovakia as the war ended) was practically the last coherent and undefeated German formation at the end of the war. It is remarkable really that, given the total collapse of Nazi Germany, they still had army units offering stern resistance even at the end.

(126) Generaloberst Franz Halder said that no German plan for the defence of Berlin ever existed.

(127) On the first day of D-Day, 83,000 British and Canadian and 70,000 American soldiers alighted on French soil. 24,000 of these troops landed by parachute or glider.

(128) 25% of the population of Byelorussia died in the Second World War.

(129) When the Allies established themselves in France after D-Day, (the Supreme Allied Commander) General Eisenhower

decided on a broad front strategy. Field Marshal Montgomery argued for a single concentrated thrust into Germany (which, of course, he proposed that he would command). Eisenhower and Montgomery soon fell out because of Montgomery's criticisms of Eisenhower's strategy.

(130) Because he was in command of a vast army made up of different nationalities, General Eisenhower had to be a diplomat as much as a soldier. This was good training for the career in politics he later had.

(131) Late in 1941, a special train was prepared for Stalin in case the Germans reached Moscow. The train would have taken Stalin to the Urals.

(132) Hitler always resisted any suggestion of using biological weapons. It is believed that part of this stemmed from his experiences of being gassed in the First World War. A fear of similar retaliation from the powerful enemies ranged against Germany was also a factor.

(133) General Blumentritt said that Adolf Hitler was no genius when it came to military strategy. He said Hitler never understood what was realistic and what wasn't. As a consequence, Hitler would often issue orders that were impossible to actually carry out.

(134) The Second World War lasted for a total of 2,174 days.

(135) The atomic bomb dropped on Hiroshima destroyed 63% of the city's buildings. Around 140,000 people were killed.

(136) The B-29 pilot carrying the atom bomb destined for Nagasaki almost ran out of runway on Tinian island. If he had crashed the island would have been destroyed.

(137) It is not known exactly how many Hitler Youth fought in the Battle for Berlin at the end of the war. Some of these children and teenagers were fanatical in their resistance.

(138) The Red Army lost 800 tanks in the battle for Berlin.

(139) A problem for German generals on the western front was that their soldiers had no fear of surrendering to the Americans or British. The eastern front was another matter entirely. No one wanted to surrender to the Red Army.

(140) British soldiers were quite fond of their army rations. Staples were Bully Beef (basically a tin of corned beef) and Hard Tack (which was like a cross between a biscuit a bread roll).

(141) British soldiers were not so fond of their toilet paper ration. They were given three sheets of toilet paper a day. American troops had a much better deal. They were permitted twenty sheets of toilet paper a day.

(142) The Germans were constantly designing new tanks, shells, and turrets in their attempt to master the situation in the east. This was counter productive in the end because all the different parts made repairing tanks more time consuming and complex.

(143) Famous actors who served in World War 2 include Jimmy Stewart, Dirk Bogarde, Walter Matthau, and David Niven,

(144) Time magazine selected Adolf Hitler as their man of the year in 1938. That's a choice they'd probably prefer to forget.

(145) In his War Diaries, Field Marshal Alan Brooke (who was the head of the British Army and Churchill's most senior military advisor) said that he would have had no hesitation in deploying poison gas on the beaches in the event of a German invasion of Britain.

(146) D-Day was a tremendous logistical feat because it took 45 troop ships to transport a single division.

(147) Near the end of the war, General Heinrici ignored an order from Hitler for Army Group Vistula to defend Berlin and save him. Heinrici kept what was left of his army group out of Berlin because he felt further fighting was pointless and would only kill more civilians. Heinrici's main concern was for his soldiers to surrender to the Allies rather than the Red Army.

(149) Hermann Göring, the head of the Luftwaffe, had a large portion of the blame for the loss of the Sixth Army at Stalingrad. Göring's promise to supply the Sixth Army through air drops proved hopelessly optimistic and unrealistic. Nowhere near enough food or ammunition ever got to the besieged army.

(150) In the Battle of Stalingrad, German soldiers would sometimes find sentries in the morning who had frozen to death in the position they had been standing.

(151) After his surrender at Stalingrad, (an understandably bitter) Friedrich von Paulus allowed himself to be used as a Soviet propaganda tool and made no secret of the fact that he despised Hitler. Hitler had refused to allow the Sixth Army to try and fight their way out of Stalingrad back to German lines. This essentially doomed 250,000 men to death or captivity.

(152) By the end of the war, the United States was supplying 47% of the weapons used by the countries in the British Commonwealth.

(153) Rudolf Hess was Hitler's deputy. In May 1941 he flew to Scotland alone to seek peace between Britain and Germany. He was detained and later tried at the Nuremberg trials. Hess was sent to Spandau Prison in west Berlin and died behind bars in 1987. The strange Hess affair was bewildering and a great embarrassment for Hitler. It is speculated that Hess was suffering from mental illness.

(154) General de Gaulle, leader of the Free French, tried to get

himself into France as fast as possible and claim as much credit for anything he could after D-Day because he was fearful that the French Resistance might attempt to run France themselves after the war.

(155) The conduct of the Red Army was brutal and grim when it reached German soil. The Soviets seemed to regard any women they found as a right of conquest and rape was common.

(156) President Roosevelt was confined to a wheelchair but most Americans were unaware of this because the wheelchair was always hidden when he appeared in newsreel footage.

(157) The US Seventh Army and the French First Army took six hundred thousand prisoners in the Alps in April 1945.

(158) General Patton was once ordered to go around the town of Trier because army intelligence calculated it would take four entire divisions to capture it. Patton cabled back that he had already captured Trier with two divisions and (sarcastically) asked if they wanted him to give it back to the Germans.

(159) Although banned by the Geneva convention, the Allies had stockpiles of chemical weapons in case the Nazis used them first.

(160) One of the best Soviet commanders was Marshal Konstantin Rokossovsky. Rokossovsky had major commands through the war and played important roles in Kursk and Operation Bagration. However, before the war started Rokossovsky nearly died in a gulag. He was raised in Warsaw with a Polish father and the Soviets accused him of being a spy. Rokossovsky was only saved from the gulag because the Red Army was in desperate need of competent military officers and strategists.

(161) One of the problems with the German defence of Normandy was a lack of agreement between the famous Field

Marshals Erwin Rommel and Gerd von Rundstedt. Rommel commanded an army group in France while Gerd von Rundstedt was the supreme commander of the western theatre. Both of these men thought they knew what was best and were loath to concede anything to one another. Rommel thought that an invasion could only be repulsed on the beaches and wanted all the German armour right on the coast. Gerd von Rundstedt disagreed and thought the armoured divisions should be pulled back so they could be used in a devastating surprise attack on the Allied forces who moved inland. Neither of these plans was put to the test and the German strategy became a vague muddle.

(162) Japan had 1.5 million military casualties in World War 2.

(163) The United States had 407,000 military casualties in World War 2.

(164) Sixty B-17 bombers were shot down by the Germans during a single Allied raid in August 1943.

(165) Generalfeldmarschall Walther Model, Hitler's favourite general, ended the war trapped in the Ruhr (an important industrial region of Germany) with Army Group B. When he realised the military situation was completely hopeless, Model dissolved Army Group B and went into the woods to shoot himself.

(166) At the very start of Operation Barbarossa, the Red Army was not allowed to evacuate civilians or shoot back. Stalin still hoped the invasion was simply a false alarm and didn't want to provoke the Germans.

(167) The Soviet Union bore the brunt of the fighting in World War 2 and played by far the biggest role in defeating Hitler. However, modern Russia tends to gloss over the fact that Stalin signed a pact with Nazi Germany in 1939 to carve up eastern Europe between them.

(168) Some Russian historians claim that Stalin was preparing an attack on western Europe and Germany when Operation Barborossa was launched. While this is debatable, it does seem very plausible that Stalin would have attacked Germany at some point if Hitler hadn't invaded first.

(169) Guderian's Panzer Group actually got within sight of Moscow. The German generals believed that a single concentrated strike on Moscow should have been adopted rather than the broad front strategy of Hitler.

(170) Operation Dynamo, the evacuation at Dunkirk, retrieved 193,000 British and 145,000 French troops. This was way beyond the exceptions of the authorities because they feared they would only be able to rescue 40,000 men.

(171) The RAF had 1,960 aircraft at its disposal in July 1940. This was less than the Luftwaffe had available.

(172) 40,000 American airmen were killed in combat in World War 2.

(173) The loss of the Sixth Army at Stalingrad was a shattering blow for Hitler and Nazi propaganda. The Sixth Army was the most powerful formation the Germans had.

(174) Hitler apparently had a strange belief that the country in control of Prague would always control Europe.

(175) The Germans lost 1,887 aircraft in the Battle of Britain.

(176) The Allied bombing of Dresden (Operation Thunderclap) was controversial and harrowing. The bombs created a firestorm which left ten of thousands of charred bodies in the street. In the British parliament, Churchill came under fire for the strategy of 'terror bombing' cities at random. The reason why the Allied bombing of German cities like Dresden was morally questionable is that the war was practically won by this stage anyway.

(177) The German air defences were so poor by the time of Dresden that many flak guns were made of papier mache and simply an illusion to make it look as if there were ground defences.

(178) When General Patton was introduced to the wives of his officers at a function, he told the wives they were going to make beautiful widows.

(179) Hermann Göring was a very powerful figure in the Nazi court at first but his power declined because of the impotence of the Luftwaffe later in the war. Göring had once proclaimed that no bombs would ever be dropped on Germany. This obviously turned out to be a preposterous and ridiculously inaccurate statement.

(180) When the German troops took up their positions on the eastern frontier in preparation for Operation Barbarossa, Stalin dismissed the talk of invasion as a plot by Winston Churchill to get the Soviet Union to enter the war on Britain's side.

(181) Poland had 70,000 men killed, 133,000 wounded and 700,000 captured in their attempt to defend the country from the invasion by Nazi Germany.

(182) Although the Spitfire fighter plane is an iconic legend in Britain, the RAF's Hawker Hurricane actually shot down more German planes.

(183) The Germans were surprised when they encountered the excellent Soviet T-34 tank. The Germans had wrongly assumed the Red Army would have primitive technology that was inferior to their own.

(184) In the middle of 1944, the United States airforce had over two and a half million personnel and 80,000 aircraft. That dwarfs the size of the modern US air force.

(185) The border of Poland today is basically a border agreed by Churchill and Stalin over a brandy.

(186) Gerd von Rundstedt said after the war the Ardennes Offensive was a stupid idea that had absolutely nothing to do with him.

(187) The Soviet Union maintained a Far Eastern Front early in the war that had 25 Divisions and 9 Brigades. This force was in case of a Japanese attack. When it became clear that the Japanese no longer had any interest in attacking the Soviet Union, the Far Eastern Front was used as reserve to help save Moscow from the Germans. The existence of this huge reserve force came as an unpleasant surprise to the Germans.

(188) The Soviet army included penal battalions who were sometimes used to clear minefields.

(189) When Soviet prisoners were liberated by the Red Army in their tens of thousands at the end of the war they were often then sent to detention camps by Stalin for the high crime of having been captured by the Germans.

(190) Field Marshal Erwin Rommel was known as the Desert Fox because of his exploits with the Africa Korps in North Africa.

(191) London was bombed for 57 consecutive nights from September 1940.

(192) German bombing raids on Britain killed around 60,000 people. Berlin alone lost this amount of people from Allied bombing raids later in the war.

(193) The Battle of Kursk was the largest tank battle in history. It was fought during July and August 1943. Nearly one million German soldiers and over 2,000 German tanks were deployed but worn down by the intricate defensive fortifications of the

Red Army. The (only recently rebuilt) German Panzer force in the east suffered catastrophic damage in a ten day battle.

(194) Some historians have argued that the popular depiction of the German Army in World War 2 as highly modern and mobile is not really accurate. They point out that most German Divisions relied on horses and wagons.

(195) There were around seven million foreign slave labourers in Germany near the end of the war.

(196) The Germans lost half a million men in the fighting at Kursk.

(197) The United States made twelve million rifles in the duration of the war.

(198) Gerd von Rundstedt said that, when he was commanding a Germany Army Group in the Soviet Union, he and his officers once laughed out loud when they received a preposterous order from Hitler to capture a specific city immediately. The city in question was seven hundred miles away.

(199) Generalfeldmarschall Erich von Manstein is considered by many to be the best German strategist of the war. He won some remarkable victories in the Soviet Union but eventually fell out with Hitler. Manstein liked to use tactical retreats as a way to lure the Red Army into traps but Hitler had a pathological aversion to retreats and the two men clashed once too often. Hitler relieved Manstein of his duties in March 1943 and the general sat out the rest of the war.

(200) After the war and his release from prison, Erich von Manstein wrote a book called Lost Victories in which he suggested he might have won the war in the east if Hitler had left him alone. Near the end of his life, the West German government consulted Manstein on military affairs.

(201) American submarines sank 4.8 million tons of Japanese merchant shipping in the war.

(202) When the United States entered the war it had the seventh largest army in the world.

(203) When Germany invaded the Soviet Union, SS Einsatzgruppen went in behind the troops. SS Einsatzgruppen were death squads. Their orders were to kill any undesirables. The undesirables were mostly Jews and Red Army officials. These SS death squads were brutal and without any semblance of humanity. They would take photographs of their atrocities and pin them on their barrack walls.

(204) It was very difficult for the SS to hide their identity at the end of the war because all SS men had a tattoo of their blood group near the armpit. Because of this (and their fanatical Nazism), the Waffen SS were the most dogged and tenacious opponents for the Red Army at the end of the war. They simply didn't want to surrender.

(205) When Hitler flew in to visit Manstein in the Soviet Union in 1943, T-34 tanks once got within firing range of the airfield he had flown in on.

(206) The American Lend Lease scheme supplied the Red Army with 80,000 trucks in 1943.

(207) The Battle of Kursk was the first battle in the east where the Soviets had more planes in the sky than the Germans. This was a clear sign that the tide had turned.

(208) The Germans lost 3,000 tanks at the Battle of Kursk.

(209) One of the reasons why Operation Sea Lion (the Nazi invasion of Britain) didn't happen is that German intelligence estimated that Britain had 39 divisions to defend the country. This was a gross over inflation of the real number.

(210) Over half the Jewish population of Germany managed to escape before Hitler banned Jewish emigration and began the holocaust. The lucky ones were those who went to Britain or escaped from Europe altogether. The unlucky ones were those who fled to countries the Nazis were about to invade.

(211) Some historians argue that the Second World War really began in 1931 with the Japanese invasion of Manchuria.

(212) The Allies knew of Auschwitz from 1942. Some historians think the Allies should have bombed the camp - or at least the rail lines that ferried prisoners in. The US War Refugee Board once proposed that arms should be dropped into concentration camps in the hope of provoking an uprising but nothing came of this.

(213) Eisenhower refused to race the Red Army to Berlin and get his armies as eastwards as possible because an agreement to split Germany into occupied zones was already in place. Some historians think this was a political gaffe but it is hard to see how the Allies could have saved eastern Europe with millions of Soviet troops already there.

(214) During the war in the east, Hitler once ordered a fantastic concentration of tanks into a town. When the armoured units and tanks got into a complete muddle and huge traffic jam in this town, Hitler ordered the corps commander to be court martial-ed and only backed down when he was diplomatically reminded that he had given the stupid order for all these tanks to enter the town in the first place!

(215) The plan for the German invasion of Britain involved capturing Portsmouth and Dover in the first wave and then isolating London. Rundstedt said after the war that Germany never had sufficient landing craft or paratroopers to make any invasion of Britain successful.

(216) The Germans lost 1,400 planes at the Battle of Kursk.

(217) German generals knew of the extermination of the Jews and raised no objections. Even the likes of Manstein and Gerd von Rundstedt signed declarations and orders supporting the persecution and 'punishment' of the Jews.

(218) The great heavyweight champion boxer Joe Louis was used as a valuable propaganda weapon during the war. He served in a still segregated US Army, posed for endless photo calls in uniform, and donated purses to war charities. The IRS and US government later made Louis destitute though by slapping him with a huge bill for back taxes. Most people think that the debts of Joe Louis, who was a genuine American hero, should have been written off by the government.

(219) James Bond author Ian Fleming was in charge of 30 Assault Unit, a commando force that was deployed behind German lines. He also advised the United States on setting up the OSS, the precursor to the CIA. By the end of the war, Ian Fleming was a Commander - just like James Bond.

(220) The encirclement of Sixth Army at Stalingrad was only the start of an even more ambitious plan by the Soviets. Operation Saturn as designed not just to capture the Sixth Army but the entire German Army Group on the Don that it belonged to. The Germans eventually had to save the Army Group and this meant the sacrifice of Sixth Army.

(221) German soldiers were very constricted by the air superiority of the Allies after D-Day. It often became impossible for German formations to move in daylight because they would simply become a target for Allied planes.

(222) The highest ranking casualty of 'friendly fire' in the war was Lieutenant General Lesley McNair. McNair, an American officer, was killed by the US Army Air Corps.

(223) British soldiers had to burn down Bergen-Belsen concentration camp to stop the spread of typhus.

(224) The swastika is an ancient sun symbol and can be found in many old religions like Buddhism and Hinduism. The symbol means good fortune. The Nazis obviously ruined this symbol forever by adopting it.

(225) When the Allies reached the Rhine, it seemed to be a rite or custom to urinate in the river. Winston Churchill and General Patton both urinated in the Rhine.

(226) Finnish sniper Simo Häyhä killed 542 Soviets during the Winter War. The most remarkable thing about this is that he had no scope on his rifle.

(227) Only one out of every nine kamikaze pilots actually hit the target.

(228) US Marines in the Pacific used the Navajo language as a code because they knew it would bamboozle the Japanese.

(229) German soldiers were given a methamphetamine called Pervitin to give them energy and endurance.

(230) Allied soldiers used the amphetamine Benzedrine to stay awake.

(231) Operation Downfall was the name of the proposed invasion of Japan by the Allies. This never happened in the end because Japan surrendered after two atomic strikes. Operation Downfall would have required six million men to carry out.

(232) The Germans and Americans used active-IR night vision during the war.

(233) The famous Dracula actor Christopher Lee was an intelligence officer during World War 2 in the Long Range Desert Patrol missions which formed the basis of the SAS. He had actually volunteered for the 1939/40 Finnish Winter War

(when the Soviet Union invaded Finland and despite outnumbering the Fins in terms of soldiers, tanks and aircraft to a preposterous degree had a nightmarishly difficult campaign) prior to North Africa. He was also an RAF pilot until an eye injury grounded him. Lee took part in the Allied campaign in Italy too and climbed Mount Vesuvius three days before it erupted. He was at the Battle of Monte Cassino and also served in Churchill's Special Operations Executive - an elite organisation involved in espionage, sabotage and reconnaissance in Nazi dominated Europe. The unofficial name for the SOE was The Ministry of Ungentlemanly Warfare. The SOE's activities are still classified and so Lee would never speak about his time serving with them. When the war ended, the multi-lingual Christopher Lee hunted Nazis for the Central Registry of War Criminals and Security Suspects before turning his hand to acting at the age of 25.

(234) Eugene Bullard was the first African-American fighter pilot in history.

(235) The B-17 Flying Fortress could carry 4000 pounds of explosives.

(236) Marcel Petiot was the mayor of a town in France during World War 2. He offered sanctuary to Jews fleeing the authorities and then killed them with a shot of poison. He confessed to 60 murders when the war ended and he was arrested.

(237) Hitler executed eighty-four of his generals. Most of these executions were because of political plots against the leadership.

(238) When the Kriegsmarine (German Navy) desperately attempted to take out refugees by sea late in the war, Soviet submarines mercilessly sunk anything in sight killing thousands. The sinking of the Wilhelm Gustloff was the greatest maritime disaster in history.

(239) When the Germans started to get low on manpower later in the war, teenage Luftwaffe recruits were used for hastily improvised parachute divisions.

(240) Rudolf Hess spent some time imprisoned in the Tower of London. He is the last person ever to be a prisoner there.

(241) Wernher von Braun, the man behind the Nazi rockets, was taken to America after the war and worked for NASA. He was the chief engineer for the Saturn V rocket.

(242) The Battle of the Bulge saw the Allies come under attack from German jet bombers from the first time.

(243) Hitler intended the Crimean peninsula to be cleared of foreigners and populated only by Germans. This would explain why he kept fighting there even when it made more sense to withdraw.

(244) Stalin was very insecure about his appearance and had his photographs airbrushed.

(245) Between 50 to 70 million people died during World War 2.

(246) One and a half million people served in the Canadian armed forces in the war.

(247) Canadian soldiers were stationed in Britain as early as 1939.

(248) A Gurkha soldier named Havildar Lachhiman Gurung defended his post alone for four hours against the Japanese. He killed 31 Japanese soldiers in the end. The incredible thing about this is that Gurung did it all with one hand after his other hand was blown off in an explosion.

(249) The US Medal of Honor was awarded to 464 people. 266 of these had been killed in the war.

(250) When Germany was being battered from all sides late in the war, Hitler used to drive his generals mad by insisting that besieged, damaged, or retreating divisions should hold firm and form themselves into Festungs (Fortresses). Hitler's generals thought this was a stupid idea because it just took soldiers out of the battle and left them trapped.

(251) Stories of Waffen SS recruits balancing live grenades on their heads to gain nerves of steel are apocryphal.

(252) It sounds simplistic but one of the principle reasons why Nazi Germany fought on for so long was that it genuinely couldn't think of anything else to do. The thought of surrendering to the Soviets terrified them and the Allied insistence on unconditional surrender allowed Hitler and Goebbels to claim that this would mean the end of Germany.

(253) The French had more tanks, men, and heavy guns than the Germans in 1940. Even so, France fell in six weeks.

(254) Hitler felt that after the conquest of the Soviet Union, Moscow would become the hub of any Bolshevist resistance or underground movement. As a consequence of this, the Nazis planned to level Moscow and flood the ruins with an artificial lake.

(255) Nazi Germany never formally declared war on Britain.

(256) The 1st SS Panzer Division, led by the young and fanatical Lieutenant-Colonel Joachim Peiper, were responsible for the Malmédy Massacre during the Ardennes Offensive. Eighty-four American prisoners were shot in a field.

(257) The Soviets trained women to be snipers. Some of their deadliest snipers were female.

(258) Generaloberst Heinz Guderian said in his memoir that he nearly came to blows with Hitler late in the war during one

of their many arguments about the eastern front.

(259) The Wannsee Conference is where the Final Solution was set in motion. This Berlin suburb was the genesis of the Holocaust.

(260) A serviceman in the US Air Corps during the war had a 70% chance of being killed in action.

(261) British scientist Robert Watson-Watt originally tried to come up with a way to destroy planes with radio waves but when this was unsuccessful his research led to the invention of radar.

(262) In the final days of the war, incidents of German soldiers opening fire on the Waffen SS were reported.

(263) The B-17 Flying Fortress had a top speed of 280 miles per hour.

(264) The Soviets had an unexpected problem in the war when they discovered their soldiers would sometimes drink the Red Army rocket fuel. They had to alter the fuel to make it less tempting.

(265) The Spitfire was the only plane in continuous production throughout the war.

(266) Britain built 132,500 aircraft in the war.

(267) The American divisions caught unaware by the Ardennes Offensive had to throw their cooks and bakers into the line in a desperate attempt to hold out.

(268) The Nazis planned to have an exhibition called Museum of An Extinct Race after their extermination of the Jews.

(269) The Nazis exterminated babies, children, and adults with mental and physical disabilities.

(270) When Hitler visited Paris after the French surrender, the French cut the cables in the Eiffel Tower lift so that any Nazi from Hitler's entourage who went there would have to walk up all the stars.

(271) The Stuka dive bombers had separate acoustic devices to make the distinctive 'screaming' sound when they plunged to drop their bombs. This was purely to terrify and intimidate the population below.

(272) The Nazis once considered deporting all German Jews to the island of Madagascar.

(273) Field Marshal Alexander was, amongst other things, the Supreme Allied Commander of the Mediterranean in World War 2. In 1920, Alexander had actually commanded German troops in Latvia during the war against Russia.

(274) The United States built nearly 50,000 Sherman tanks from 1942 to the end of the war.

(275) President Roosevelt was ferried around in Al Capone's old limousine.

(276) Hitler gave orders for Paris to be destroyed before it could be liberated by the Allies but the German commanders there ignored him.

(277) Army Group Vistula was padded out with Luftwaffe trainees and soldiers who would ordinarily be deemed too young or too old to serve with the regular army.

(278) Nutella was invented in World War 2. Because chocolate was hard to get, someone had the idea of mixing hazelnuts with it to make chocolate go further.

(279) During the Battle of Hurtgen Forest, American and German medics shared an aid station.

(280) Kamikaze translates as 'divine wind' in Japanese.

(281) Lyudmila Pavlichenko was the deadliest female soviet sniper. She clocked up 309 kills.

(282) Bibi Hartmann was the 'ace' pilot of the Luftwaffe in the war. He shot down 352 enemy planes.

(283) The Red Army is thought to have raped two million German women.

(284) Over forty thousand men from the (neutral) Republic of Ireland fought for Britain in the war against the Nazis. Believe it or not, these men were considered traitors in Ireland because they had fought on the British side.

(285) Hitler had a sweet tooth and ate a lot of chocolate and cakes. It probably explains why he had trouble with his teeth.

(286) When the Red Army found the abandoned German command post at Zossen late in the war, this huge complex was guarded by two drunk German soldiers. There was no one else left.

(287) Tsutomu Yamaguchi must qualify as one of the unluckiest men in history. He was in Hiroshima and Nagasaki when they were struck by atom bombs. Amazingly, he managed to survive.

(288) Himmler said the Final Solution was a chapter that could never be written about. He was very careful to make sure there was no documentation that traced the policy to him. In reality, Himmler was the driving force behind the implementation of the policy.

(289) The average age of soldiers in World War 2 was 26.

(290) While the U-boats are very famous, you never hear

much about British submarines in World War 2. This is because British submarines (unlike the U-boats) didn't have ample targets and so had less action. Britain had 60 submarines at the start of the war. The British submarine fleet was most active in the Far East. In June 1945, they sank two Japanese cruisers.

(291) When Benito Mussolini learned that Hitler was going to invade the Soviet Union he was desperate to have Italian participation for his own prestige and hope in a share of whatever land and gold came from victory. Italy sent a motorised corps to fight with the Germans in the Soviet Union that was later reinforced to a full Italian Army of over 200,000 men. The Italian army in the Soviet Union was destroyed by the defeat at Stalingrad. Over 80,000 were killed or captured and those that did return home were shattered both mentally and physically from their grim experiences. Italian veterans who survived the eastern front said that their weapons were unreliable and useless and that the Italian Army was poorly trained and equipped. They blamed Mussolini for sacrificing them just so that he could keep in favour with Hitler.

(292) When General McAuliffe was asked to surrender by the Germans at Bastogne during the Battle of the Bulge, his one word reply simply said 'Nuts!'

(293) Some German snipers captured after D-Day said they had refused to shoot a British military bagpiper on the beaches because they thought the man had gone insane.

(294) Operation Bernhard was a Nazi scheme to flood Britain with forged bank notes and create hyper inflation. The plan was never activated because the caves where the notes were being printed were captured by the Allies.

(295) The heaviest tank in the war was the Tiger II. This German tank weighed 68 tonnes and had 150mm of armour.

(296) An American airman named Alan Magee survived a

22,000 foot fall without a parachute during a bombing raid in Europe.

(297) 150,000 shells were fired at Leningrad during the siege.

(298) In April 1944, the Germans only had 500 combat planes on the eastern front. The Soviets had 13,000.

(299) Stenographers recorded Hitler's military conferences from 1942. In the transcripts, Hitler is always asking someone what the time is because he never wore a wristwatch.

(300) Between July 1943 and May 1944, 41 German divisions were destroyed on the eastern front.

(301) Operation Bagration lasted for sixty-eight days.

(302) At the end of Operation Bagration, the Soviets claimed to have killed 380,000 German soldiers, wounded 384,000, and captured 158,000.

(303) The Germans lost 2,000 tanks and 57,000 motor vehicles in Operation Bagration.

(304) By the end of Operation Bagration, the large and powerful German force of Army Group Centre, which was protecting the Baltic states and East Prussia, had essentially ceased to exist.

(305) Operation Bagration was timed to coincide with D-Day. Most of the Lufftwaffe in the east had been hurriedly packed off to France so the Soviets had total dominance of the sky. Hitler was learning the hard way that it is never a good idea to end up fighting a war on two fronts.

(306) At the end of Operation Bagration, the Germans were virtually back at their Operation Barbarossa starting point. All that blood and toil and now they were right back where they began!

(307) Hitler's famous bunker was in the old Chancellery. It was more cramped than the bunker in the new Chancellery but deemed safer.

(308) Hitler's bunker only had one switchboard, one radio telephone, and one transmitter. Communication with the outside world became increasingly difficult.

(309) Near the end of the war, staff in Hitler's bunker would telephone random numbers from the Berlin telephone book to see who answered. If they heard a Russian voice on the line they could gauge how close the Red Army was.

(310) 100,000 bombs were dropped on Leningrad during the siege.

(311) U-boats were really horrible to serve on. They were cramped, claustrophobic, sweaty, and smelly.

(312) General Eisenhower had a speech written and prepared in case D-Day was a failure. In this alternative speech (which thankfully never had to be delivered) Eisenhower would have accepted full responsibility for the failure as Allied Supreme Commander.

(313) Early in 1945, Allied intelligence reported that a German infantry division last seen in Holland was now fighting in Hungry. This was very significant because it was the first instance of the Germans moving divisions from the west to the east.

(314) General Patton asked to be sent to the Pacific when the war in Europe ended. The American military declined to take him up on this.

(315) The Allied alliance got a bit frayed around the edges in the west at times because the Americans didn't like Field Marshal Montgomery. They were especially annoyed when

Montgomery seemed to suggest that his British and Canadian 21st Army Group had saved the Americans in the Battle of the Bulge.

(316) The last footage taken of Hitler was him meeting some Hitler Youth boys outside his bunker. Hitler looks like a broken man. He is stooped and aged and he can't stop one of his hands from shaking. Many believe Hitler had Parkinson's disease.

(317) In the aftermath of the Ardennes Offensive, many German divisions in the west only had 8,000 men. At the start of the war their divisions would usually have around 18,000 men.

(318) D-Day was very difficult when it came to choosing a date for the invasion because of the choppy weather in the English channel. The Allies needed all the elements to be in their favour if the operation was to succeed.

(319) General Slim, the commander of the Fourteenth Army in Burma, once ordered an airstrike on his Japanese counterpart to be cancelled. Slim could predict every decision the Japanese commander made on the battlefield and so wanted him to stay alive and remain in his post.

(320) A surprising number of German officers near the end of the war seemed to believe that the Allies were going to attack the Red Army and ask for German assistance in this operation. It was a delusional fantasy.

(321) In the west after D-Day, the German 70th Infantry Division in Holland was made up entirely of men with gastric and stomach complaints. They were nicknamed the White Bread Division.

(322) Hitler never once visited a bomb site in Germany during the entire war.

(323) The Allies dropped 2.7 million tons of bombs on Europe in the war. Half of these bombs were dropped on Germany.

(324) To this day, 2,000 tons of unexploded bombs are still discovered in Germany each year.

(325) The Soviet 13th Guards Rifle Division protected the city and landing zones when Stalingrad was under attack. They went in with 10,000 men and by the time they were relieved only 320 of those 10,000 men were still alive.

(326) Unit 731 was a covert biological and chemical warfare research and development unit of the Imperial Japanese Army. It was responsible for horrific torture and experimentation on live people. Most of the victims were Chinese. People were frozen, raped, had organs removed while they were alive, and were even used as live targets to test weapons. Believe it or not, General Douglas MacArthur gave the leader and staff of Unit 731 immunity and swept it under the carpet so that the Americans could gather the Japanese research on chemical and biological weapons. Those involved in Unit 731 should have been put on trial like the Nazi war criminals.

(327) 41% of Canadian men aged 16-45 served in the military during World War 2.

(328) Canada had the third largest navy in the world at the end of the war.

(329) Studies have shown that 4% of the sand on the Normandy beaches still consists of shrapnel.

(330) The life expectancy for a Red Army soldier defending Stalingrad at the height of the fighting was one day. If you survived longer than 24 hours it was a miracle.

(331) Hitler spared Oxford from German bombing raids because he wanted the city to be the capital of Nazi Britain.

(332) The Soviets had some female bomber pilots.

(333) Iceland was neutral in the war and refused to join the Allies. Because of its strategic location though, the British sent Royal Marines to Iceland to cut communications, guard the ports, and arrest the German diplomatic presence.

(334) A lot of black Free French soldiers were airbrushed out of victory parades at the end of the war.

(335) Paul Tibbets, the pilot who flew the atom bomb to Hiroshima, asked not to have a grave or headstone after his death in case it was targeted by nuclear protesters.

(336) 200, 000 civilians were slaughtered by the Nazis during the Warsaw Uprising. It is often suggested that Stalin paused the Red Army offensive to allow the Nazis to crush resistance in Warsaw.

(337) When the American Army began flooding into Britain for D-Day, British pubs and cafes were bemused by the American policy of segregation between white and black soldiers.

(338) It was quite common in World War 2 for the Allies to use dummy inflatable tanks to deceive the enemy as to their actual position.

(339) The Germans controlled over 90% of Stalingrad at one point.

(340) The Attack on Mers-el-Kébir took place in 1940. This concerned the French naval fleet in French Algeria. The British were concerned that these ships would fall into the hands of Germany now that France had been defeated. Despite assurances from Admiral François Darlan, commander of the French Navy, that this would not happen, Winston Churchill ordered an attack on the French ships. Six ships were sunk or

damaged and over a thousand French navy personnel were killed. Churchill said it was the most difficult decision he had to make during the war. Roosevelt later told Churchill that he would have done the same thing. The French were infuriated by the action. They even tried to bomb Gibraltar in retaliation.

(341) Brazil was the only South American country to have ground troops fighting for the Allies in Europe.

(342) Seven hundred people a day died during the Siege of Leningrad.

(343) During the Battle of the Bulge, the Germans had English speaking units dressed in American uniforms who were supposed to get behind Allied lines and create havoc. The American sentries would therefore ask baseball questions in order to test if soldiers were really American or just Germans in American uniforms.

(344) The United States deployed a military force in World War 2 thirty times larger than the force they deployed in the Vietnam War.

(345) All the German spies sent to Britain were turned into double-agents.

(346) The Soviet Union lost over 300,000 men in the Winter War. Finland lost 70,000.

(347) The Germans weren't the only ones to have jet fighters before the war ended. The British Gloster Meteor saw limited action in the war.

(348) The island of Malta had 14,000 bombs dropped on it during the war.

(349) The French destroyed over half of the German tanks and planes that attacked them during the Battle of France.

(350) The Battle of El Alamein was fought in October and November 1942 near the Egyptian railway halt of El Alamein. The British Eighth Army of Montgomery defeated the Africa Korps of Rommel. The victory stopped the Middle Eastern and Persian oil fields from falling into Axis hands.

(351) Otto Skorzeny was an Austrian SS-Standartenführer in the Waffen SS. He became known as Hitler's personal commando. Skorzeny was essentially special forces before that term became well known. Skorzeny was the man who rescued Mussolini from partisans in a glider raid. He was also in charge of Operation Griffin (Unternehmen Greif) at the Battle of the Bulge. This was the deception of German soldiers pretending to be American troops.

(352) The Waffen SS were initially created to be Hitler's elite private bodyguard but by 1944 they had nearly a million soldiers fighting in the war. After the plots against him, Hitler distrusted the regular army. This is why the Waffen SS got the 'prima donna' role in the failed Ardennes Offensive.

(353) General Patton called the Soviets 'recently civilised Mongolian bandits' at the end of the war and seemed to suggest that America should now fight the Red Army.

(354) Mussolini blamed his generals and the Germans for the Italians surrendering in huge numbers and being pushed out of North Africa. He claimed to have been mislead about fortifications and battles. The Germans, he claimed, never provided enough equipment. Never once did he blame himself for getting the Italian Army into this mess in the first place!

(355) There was a huge contribution made to the British Army by Indian and African troops.

(356) Many German generals wanted a limited war with conquests that would be easy to defend or maintain. Hitler however wanted living space in the east.

(357) Hermann Göring's brother hated the Nazis and helped Jewish people escape.

(358) Stalin gave the Ukraine priority because it would restore the agricultural and mineral resources of the area back to Soviet control and also put his army a footstep away from eastern Europe. Hitler also wanted to retain control of the region for many of the same reasons but also because if it was lost the Soviet Union would then be within striking distance of the Rumanian oil fields that kept the German war machine running.

(359) The vast alien terrain of the Soviet Union was deeply alienating to a lot of German soldiers. The sheer expanse of nothingness affected them on an existential level.

(360) Hitler would fly into a rage whenever he was presented with reports of Soviet factories producing more than German ones.

(361) A British plan to kill Hitler by sniper in 1944 was codenamed Operation Foxley. The plan was scrapped because the Allies felt it was better for them to have a poor strategist like Hitler in charge of the German armed forces.

(362) Winston Churchill was in his private cinema watching a Marx Brothers film when he was told that Rudolph Hess had landed in Scotland. Churchill decided to finish watching the film rather than concern himself with Hess.

(363) German magnetic mines accounted for 800,000 tons of British shipping even before the U-boat campaign began.

(364) The French had more tanks than the Germans in the Battle of France but the French tanks were scattered and dispersed. The German tanks were concentrated at focal points and so much more effective.

(365) It is often speculated that Hitler halted his panzer

divisions at Dunkirk because he thought letting the British escape would make them more amenable to a peace deal. The more common theory is that the panzer divisions simply needed a rest after all the fighting they had done and the Germans assumed the Luftwaffe alone would finish off the British.

(366) The Germans levied a tax on France to make the French pay for the German army of occupation.

(367) British and German soldiers did not fire a shot at each other between June 1940 and March 1941. During this period the war between the countries was conducted at sea and in the air.

(368) Hitler was so confident of defeating the Soviet Union in swift fashion that German munitions production was cut by 40% in the autumn of 1941.

(369) The Allied landings at Normandy required over 4000 landing craft.

(370) Allied planes crippled the French railway system before D-Day. The German Army was reliant on trains for their supplies so this was a vital target.

(371) The French Resistance offered to sabotage the French railway system for the Allies because it would mean less civilian casualties. The Allies ignored this offer.

(372) The American estimated that they might endure a million casualties in any invasion of Japan. It was fully expected that the Japanese would fight tenaciously to the last bullet.

(373) When Hitler invaded the Soviet Union, no one thought that the Soviets could hold out for long. British intelligence thought the war would effectively be over in ten days. Roosevelt's advisors told him that the Red Army would only be

able to offer resistance for about a month.

(374) At the end of the war, Winston Churchill asked his military chiefs to draft a report on whether or not it would be feasible, should Stalin renege on his promises, to throw the Red Army out of eastern Europe with a surprise attack. The report, which was called Operation Unthinkable, concluded that even with American help this would be impossible. The Soviets had twice as many troops in Europe than the Allies.

(375) The Germans never had much of a surface fleet in the war. Hitler never seemed very interested in naval warfare. He once said he was a hero on land and a coward on water.

(376) The American commanders in the Pacific didn't want any other Allied countries to be involved in the proposed invasion of Japan. In the end though it was agreed that a British and Australian naval fleet and army corps would take part. The invasion never happened though because of the atom bombs dropped on Japan. The American desire not to have other Allies involved in the invasion of Japan was mostly because of logistics.

(377) During the war, things like butter, meat, cheese, and chocolate were rationed in Britain and people were encouraged to 'dig for victory' and grow their own vegetables. Cases of heart disease and illness declined during this period. Despite (or rather BECAUSE of) rationing, people were actually very healthy.

(378) Hitler's stubbornness when it came to his refusal to sanction withdrawals or retreats (even when they made military sense) may have stemmed from his experiences of the First World War. Hitler said that retreats in the First World War always destroyed morale.

(379) D-Day required 864 Allied transport ships.

(380) The Allied invasion of Sicily took place eleven months

before D-Day. Eisenhower was anxious about this invasion because the Allies had never staged an opposed amphibious landing before.

(381) 150,000 Allied troops land on the first day of the Sicily invasion. They required 300 landing craft.

(382) The Soviet infantry could advance for weeks at a time with no supplies. They would eat raw vegetables from the fields.

(383) The Allies got 156,000 men ashore by the time evening arrived on D-Day.

(384) The Germans came up with the first assault rifle during the war.

(385) Remarkably, despite the Allied bombing raids, Germany produced more munitions than ever in 1944.

(386) Operation Barbarossa was eventually hamstrung by vague strategic goals. Hitler often seemed to be making it up as he went along. This strategic 'drift' allowed the army groups to become too scattered and dispersed.

(387) The Mustang fighter had a range of a thousand miles. This made it a perfect escort for bombing missions.

(388) The V-1 rocket destroyed 25,000 houses in Britain.

(389) The Battle of Midway was devastating for the Japanese because it left them with the same amount of carriers as the United States. Several months later, the United States had nineteen carriers and the Japanese had ten. The balance of power in the Pacific had shifted.

(390) The Luftwaffe required 160,000 tons of fuel a month to be fully operational. By September 1944, they had to get by on only 10,000 tons of fuel a month. This is why the Luftwaffe

became so impotent later in the war. They simply didn't have enough fuel or trained pilots anymore.

(391) When he first became active in politics, one of Hitler's colleagues told him to shave off his toothbrush mustache because it looked stupid. Hitler refused to do this.

(392) The fall of France was a disaster for the Allies at sea because it meant the German U-boats could now be launched from the French Atlantic ports.

(393) In a transcript of one of Hitler's military conferences not long before D-Day, Hitler repeatedly requested that more flamethrowers should be sent to the German Army in France. Hitler seemed very excited by flamethrowers.

(394) The Allies towed two artificial harbours, called Mullberries, across the channel as part of D-Day.

(395) The famous writer JD Salinger served in the 12th US Infantry Regiment of the 4th Infantry Division in World War 2. Salinger was at Utah Beach on D-Day and saw action at the Battle of the Bulge and the Huertgen Forest campaign. Salinger was also there when the Americans entered the concentration camp at Dachau and said the smell of burning flesh was impossible to ever forget. Salinger is believed to have started writing (what later became) The Catcher in the Rye in foxholes while in Europe.

(396) Blitzkrieg translates as lightning war. The Germans gave this term to the concentration of mobile tank divisions with close air support. The combination of speed and concentrated firepower was designed to win quick decisive victories before the enemy knew what hit them.

(397) Winston Churchill called Italy the 'soft underbelly' of the Axis crocodile but the Allies found this was far from the case when they invaded. The rain turned all to mud and made any movement a struggle and the Germans used the terrain to fight

a brilliant defensive campaign.

(398) George Marshall, American general of the army, was the chief of staff of the US Army during the war. As chief of staff, Marshall increased the Army from a strength of around 200,000 to almost 8.5 million.

(399) Operation Market Garden took place in September 1944. It was the largest airborne military operation in history and supposed to cut the German position at Arnhem and pave the way for a crossing of the Rhine. The operation was designed to end the war early by capturing the Ruhr, shortening the Allied supply lines, and allowing for a crossing of the Rhine. The operation was not a success. The biggest disaster for the Allies was that the Germans had two SS Panzer Divisions (they were unaware of) in a crucial position. The British 1st Airborne Division were dropped 60 miles behind German lines but were then surrounded and heavily outnumbered in the end.

(400) When the British 1st Airborne Division were fighting in Operation Market Garden, the Germans allowed the besieged British soldiers to evacuate their injured men. This is not something you could imagine the Germans doing on the eastern front.

(401) Near the end of the war, disillusioned German soldiers had a joke which, when translated, went something like this - 'If you can see silver aircraft, they are American, if you can see khaki planes, they are British, and if you can't see any planes, then they're German.'

(402) The men of the US Eighth Air Force were expected to complete 25 combat missions before they allowed to go home. The chances of being killed before you completed 25 missions was 86%.

(403) The Channel Islands were the only part of the British Isles to be occupied by the Nazis during the war. These islands are close to northern France and were impossible to defend

once France fell.

(404) The theory that Hitler was smuggled out of Berlin to South America on a U-boat and spent the last years of his life living in Argentina has spawned a number of books and TV shows. The Allied authorities kept an open mind on this theory themselves for a time when the war had ended. However, the evidence for this theory is scant to say the least. The theory states that Hitler was smuggled to the Spanish coast and taken to Argentina on a U-boat. From all that we know about Hitler, he didn't exactly seem like the sort of person who would shave his hair off and go and live in the jungle as a fugitive!

(405) Near the end of the war, General Busse's battered Ninth German Army undertook a harrowing trek with civilians to try and get away from the Red Army and surrender to the western Allies. In 1999 the Ninth Army's Enigma machine was discovered in a shallow grave near an autobahn.

(406) Operation Tiger was an Allied training exercise for D-Day that took place on the beaches of Devon in England. Some Nazi submarines noticed the Allied ships taking part in the exercise and attacked them. 70 Americans were killed in the attack. The Allied authorities kept this all secret at the time because they didn't want anything to damage morale before D-Day.

(407) Operation Countenance was the August 1941 invasion of Iran by Britain and the Soviet Union. Churchill and Stalin feared that Iran was about to have a pro-Axis leadership and so they invaded the country. The invasion met with minimal resistance. This was a rare instance of Britain and the Soviet Union fighting as an Allied force together in the same area.

(408) Operation Mincemeat was a deception by the British to misdirect the Nazis about Allied intentions regarding Sicily. The corpse of a hobo was taken from a morgue and dressed in a British military uniform handcuffed to a briefcase with (fictitious) plans for an Allied invasion of Greece. The body

was placed on the south coast of Spain and - incredibly - the ruse worked. The Spanish picked up the body and told the Germans. Hitler then transferred some divisions to Greece.

(409) The Nazis looted gold panels worth hundreds of millions of dollars today from the Amber Room at the Tsarskoye Selo Palace in St Petersburg in Russia.

(410) In 2005, 88 year-old Italian author Luigi Romersa said that, during the war, he saw the Nazis detonate a small nuclear bomb on the island of Rügen off the north coast of Germany.

(411) 35,000 Allied prisoners of war escaped from German and Italian camps during World War 2.

(412) 20% of the Battle of Britain fighter pilots defending Britain were foreign. They included Czechs, Poles, West Indians, and Americans.

(413) Stalin was said to be a big fan of cowboy films.

(414) Martin Bormann was the Nazi Party Secretary and more or less Hitler's number two by the end of the war (Joseph Goebbels is the only other Nazi who could claim to have been as close to Hitler right to the bitter end). Hitler and Goebbels killed themselves in the bunker when the Red Army reached Berlin but Bormann tried to escape. There were, for many decades, attempts to find Bormann or deduce what happened to him. In the 1980s though, DNA from bones found in Berlin proved that Bormann had died near the bunker. He obviously hadn't got very far at all in his attempt to escape.

(415) The Nazis took 50,000 Polish babies back to Germany. The babies were given new families and brought up as Germans.

(416) The Brazilian Expeditionary Force took 20,573 Axis prisoners during the Italian campaign.

(417) Japanese kamikaze pilots destroyed around 300 ships.

(418) Queen Elizabeth II was a mechanic in the British Army during World War 2.

(419) In May 1945, at Itter in the Austrian Alps, American and German soldiers fought the SS to rescue prominent French prisoners of war. This was the only instance of only Americans and Germans fighting together.

(420) The Karl-Gerät (Mörser Karl) was the biggest field gun of the war. This German gun weighed 137 tons and required a crane and railway tracks to move around. It was used in attacking the Soviet fortresses of Brest-Litovsk and Sevastopol and also saw action during the Battle of the Bulge. Because of its extreme size, only seven of these guns were built.

(421) 20,351 Spitfires were produced in the war.

(422) The Ilyushin Il-2 was a Soviet ground attack aircraft. 36,000 of these were built in the war - making it the most mass produced aircraft of the conflict.

(423) The worst Japanese atrocity (and there were many Japanese atrocities during the war) was the Nanking Massacre, in which 50 to 300 thousand Chinese civilians were raped and murdered.

(424) American prisoners of war under the Japanese had a death rate of 37%. This was much worse than the death rate for American soldiers who were prisoners of the Germans.

(425) 37,583 British prisoners were released after Japan surrendered. The Japanese also released 14,473 American prisoners.

(426) In 1942, 100,000 Japanese living on the west coast of the United States were interned. This was a controversial move but deemed necessary by the authorities.

(427) During the Siege of Leningrad, bread was baked with cellulose, cottonseed and oats that were meant for horses.

(428) There was never any real danger of Japan invading Australia. Although the Japanese military discussed an invasion and felt that Australia was lightly defended, they judged that too much shipping would have been required to supply an army in Australia and so decided instead on a policy to isolate Australia in the region rather than direct conquest.

(429) The force that Hitler invaded the Soviet Union with wasn't that much bigger than the forces he used to invade France. Hitler thought that beating the Red Army would actually be easier than defeating the French.

(430) Stalin developed two parallel Soviet armies in the war. There was an army of quantity that was often used as canon fodder, thrown into bloody battles of attrition where the generals were perfectly happy to sacrifice thousands of lives just to affect a breakthrough somewhere. Then there were the guards armies - more elite and professional formations.

(431) The SS began recruiting foreign soldiers in 1940. The Wiking Division was the first major success. It was made up of volunteers from Scandinavia, the Low Countries and Estonia.

(432) The Germans tried to set up a British Free Corps in the SS. This would have been made up of British prisoners of war who wanted to join the fight against the Soviet Union. It never got off the ground though because the Nazis could only find 27 British POWs willing to join.

(433) German army officers disliked the Waffen SS. They were annoyed that young men and new weapons were being diverted by the growth of the Waffen SS.

(434) In his memoir, Field Marshal William Slim said that he was always dubious about the mystique and prowess afforded

to special forces. Slim believed regular soldiers were no less special.

(435) The battle of the Seelow Heights on the Oder in April 1945 was the last stand of the Germans in the east. This was about 50 or 60 miles from Berlin and the last natural geographical barrier that the Germans could use for defensive purposes with its hills and rivers. The battle only lasted for three days. 20,000 guns and rocket batteries pounded the German defenders before the numerically superior Red Army forces attacked. By the end of the battle, Army Group Vistula was battered, split, isolated, and effectively finished as a coherent fighting force.

(436) The jet-powered Messerschmitt Me 262 had a top speed of 541mph.

(437) The 88mm Gun was one of the deadliest German weapons of World War 2. It was designed as a flak gun but became an offensive weapon. It destroyed many tanks in North Africa and was used against the Red Army.

(438) The M1 Garand Rifle used by American soldiers in World War 2 was also used in the Korean War. American soldiers were the only nationality to have an auto-loading rifle in World War 2.

(439) The Germans got to within fifteen miles of Moscow. If Hitler had allocated more forces to the city and made it much more of an early priority then it is very difficult to see how the Red Army could have prevented its capture.

(440) When the Germans invaded the Soviet Union, they found that the maps they had been given were completely inaccurate. The German planners had also assumed that the Soviet Union had plenty of German style roads but this wasn't the case at all. The primitive Soviet roads made transportation very difficult.

(441) A U-boat could typically travel underwater for two hours at a time.

(442) The last German offensive in the east, and their last of the war, was Operation Spring Awakening. After the fall of Budapest, Hitler was concerned that the Red Army were only 50 miles away from the oil fields of Nagykanizsa - one of the last sources of oil left to Germany. Operation Spring Awakening was designed to throw the Soviets back over the River Danube and stabilise the situation. Waffen SS Divisions from the aborted Ardennes Offensive were sent from west to east for the offensive but it proved to be a failure. The SS Divisions got bogged down in heavy mud and the Red Army defences were too strong.

(443) Rommel was on leave when the Allies invaded on D-Day. Rommel's staff took a long time to deduce that this was a real invasion and not a false alarm.

(444) On the 7th of March, 1945, American soldiers captured an intact bridge over the Rhine at Remagen. This was a tremendous feat and a great blow to German morale.

(445) The Hawker Hurricane had a top speed of 340mph and a range of 468 miles.

(446) Waffen SS recruits carried out much of their training under live fire. This was designed to teach them to be calm and careful in a real firefight.

(447) German soldiers had woefully inadequate winter clothing for their invasion of the Soviet Union. It could fall to 50 degrees below zero at night and endless cases of frostbite were recorded.

(448) A U-boat typically carried 14 torpedoes. U-boat captains would usually try and save a few of these so that they still had a few left up their sleeve for the journey back to port.

(449) The British Commonwealth forces defending Burma were so weak at one point they only had seven planes to put in the sky. The Japanese had 230.

(450) The SS Battlegroup commanded by Joachim Peiper made the most progress in the Ardennes Offensive. Peiper abandoned the advance though because his battlegroup had nearly run out of fuel. Unknown to Peiper, the battlegroup was only two kilometres away from an American fuel dump when they stopped. If they had carried on going they would have found two million gallons of fuel.

(451) The ammunition the Germans used for their artillery barrage at the start of the Ardennes Offensive was brought up by hand to save fuel and keep noise to a minimum.

(452) U-boat is an abbreviation of Unterseeboot - which means undersea boat.

(453) Hitler believed the Ardennes Offensive would destroy 30 British and American divisions, trap Montgomery's army group on the coast, and make Canada pull out of the war. These were ludicrous expectations that had no basis in reality. It was a complete fantasy.

(454) The training for Waffen SS recruits including boxing, cross country running, weapons handling, and digging foxholes.

(455) When American sentries asked baseball questions to anyone passing through their lines during the Battle of the Bulge to flush out German impostors, they ran into the actor David Niven one night. Niven was serving with the British Army and couldn't answer any of the baseball questions. Niven had to persuade the sentries that he really WAS the actor David Niven.

(456) Hitler shot himself in the foot by firing or moving so many of his best generals. It was madness to dismiss Manstein

and fired Rundstedt twice. Model was one of Hitler's most competent generals but Hitler never left him in one place long enough for Model to have an enduring effect.

(457) When General Heinrici arrived at the headquarters of Army Group Vistula to take over from Himmler, he found that everything was decorated white with green drapes. Heinrici thought it looked more like a boudoir than a military headquarters.

(458) 1,162 U-boats were built by the Nazis before and during the war. 863 saw service and 784 were lost.

(459) As part of their indoctrination training, Waffen SS recruits were taught that Jews were Untermensch (subhuman or racially inferior) and must be shown no pity or mercy. SS recruits were told that if they showed any sympathy to the Jews whatsoever then Germany would lose the war.

(460) The indoctrination training for SS recruits was hardly necessary in many cases. Most of the recruits were fanatical and deluded Nazis to start with.

(461) A lot of the tanks lost by the Germans in the Battle of the Bulge were destroyed by the Germans themselves after they ran out of fuel.

(462) General Mark Clark was the youngest lieutenant general (three-star general) in the US Army. Clark commanded the Fifth Army in Italy and ignored his strategic orders from Allied Command so that he could be the first person to liberate Rome. Clark's (rather vain) action allowed thousands of German soldiers in the German Tenth Army to escape. The broadcaster Alan Whicker, who was in the British Army's Film and Photo Unit in Italy at the time, later said - 'After breaking out of Anzio, Alexander's plan was for the Fifth Army to drive east to cut Kesselring's escape route to the north and trap much of his Tenth and Fourteenth Armies. The operation started well, but then suddenly, when leading troops were only

six kilometres from closing their trap at Frosinone, the Fifth Army was re-directed and sent north towards Rome. The trap was left open. General Mark Clark was so eager that the world should see pictures showing him as the liberator of Rome, that he allowed the armies of a delighted Kesselring to escape. He had ignored the orders of Field Marshal Alexander in a decision as militarily stupid, as it was insubordinate. This, vain-glorious blunder, the worst of the entire war, lost us a stunning victory, lengthened the war by many months and earned Mark Clark the contempt of other American and British generals. They saw an operation that could have won the war in Italy, thrown away at the cost of many Allied lives, because of the obsession and vanity of one man. If General Mark Clark had been in the German Army, Hitler would have had him shot.'

(463) Roland Freisler was the President of the Nazi People's Court. As you can imagine, the chances of getting a fair trial at this court were precisely zero. Freisler, in his role as judge, would simply shout abuse at any defendants who ended up in his court. Freisler, an obnoxious and deranged Nazi, was killed in 1945 when the Allies bombed the court building.

(464) U-boats typically had a depth of 200 to 280 metres.

(465) Goebbels celebrated when Roosevelt died before the end of the war. Goebbels excitedly told Hitler this was a sign that their fortunes had changed.

(466) Bernard Law Montgomery became one of the most famous generals in the war after his exploits with the British Eighth Army in North Africa. It could have been different though. This command was supposed to go to Lieutenant-general William 'Strafer' Gott but Gott died in a plane crash and so Montgomery replaced him.

(467) German radio stations would broadcast propaganda aimed at a British and Allied audience during he war. These were English language broadcasts that presented a very biased

pro-Nazi take on the war. The presenter of the English language broadcasts became known as Lord Haw Haw (Jonah Barrington of the Daily Express came up with this phrase) in Britain. More than one person took the role of 'Lord Haw Haw' but the best known was William Joyce. Joyce was born in America and raised in Ireland. He was a member of the British Union of Fascists and fled to Germany to avoid being interned by the British government during the war. Joyce was happy to be a useful idiot for the Nazis and goaded Britain through German propaganda broadcasts. At the end of the war, Joyce was captured by the British Army in Germany and put on trial. When he was sentenced to death for treason, he appealed on the grounds that he was American born and not a subject of the crown. His appeal was rejected because Joyce had a British passport and had voted in British elections. William Joyce was hung in 1946 at Wandsworth Prison in London.

(468) The Germans lost on average 60,000 soldiers a month on the eastern front between 1941 and 1944.

(469) Hermann Göring was Hitler's supposed successor but was arrested by the SS near the end of the war when he assumed Hitler was cut-off in the bunker and incapable of further leadership. When Göring was in the custody of the SS, a Luftwaffe Signals Regiment marched through where he was being held. The quick-thinking Göring ordered the Luftwaffe Regiment to rescue him and so they overpowered the SS and freed their boss.

(470) In the latter stages of the war, Hitler was given a German military report that estimated in some sectors the Red Army now outnumbered the Germans by a factor of 20 to 1 in men and guns. Hitler laughed and said the author of this report should be locked up in a lunatic asylum. However, the report turned out to be completely accurate.

(471) U-boats had no showers. The men on the boats had to use strong deodorant.

(472) The Soviet railway system was completely different to the German one and German engineers had to adapt it so that German supplies could be brought to the front from their supply bases.

(473) In the event of a Nazi invasion of Britain, church bells were to ring to signify that the Germans had landed. There were one or two false alarms. A village once started ringing its church bells when wild (and inaccurate) stories of German paratroopers landing in the area abounded.

(474) President Roosevelt told his generals to make as many German civilians as possible go and look at the concentration camps so that no German in the future could ever deny that this really happened.

(475) When Germany was losing the war, Heinrich Himmler ordered concentration commandants to destroy records, crematoria, and other signs of mass extermination.

(476) Himmler was persuaded by his advisors to talk to the Swedish Red Cross about surrendering to the Allies late in the war. The Red Cross wanted Himmler to release Jewish prisoners while Himmler was simply exploring a possible means to save himself. Himmler was so divorced from reality he thought there might be a chance that he could lead a post-war Germany. In the end, Hitler heard about Himmler's tentative negotiations and ordered Himmler to be arrested. At this stage of the war thought it was difficult for any orders of Hitler to be carried out as Germany was split in two and Hitler was trapped in Berlin.

(477) When the war ended, Himmler dressed in civilian clothes and tried to disappear. He was captured by British soldiers and crunched on a cyanide capsule in custody - dying instantly.

(478) The U-boats had alkaline cartridges for air purification.

(479) The main reason the Allies were caught napping by the Ardennes Offensive is that they had assumed the Germans were no longer capable of staging big offensives at this stage of the war.

(480) In an attempt to encourage people to grow and eat vegetables during the war, the British government printed posters in which it said that if you ate carrots you would be able to spot more Nazi planes. To this day the myth that eating carrots improves your eyesight still persists.

(481) Men on U-boats had to eat mostly canned food because diesel vapor contaminated fresh produce.

(482) Hitler's personal physician Theodor Morell played a big part in the rapid deterioration of Hitler's health. Morell injected Hitler with prescriptions that included arsenic, strychine, and various unknown drugs.

(483) Hitler's health wasn't helped much either by the fact that he lived in a bunker and rarely got any sleep.

(484) When there was a threat of a Nazi invasion, a rumour got around that the British were going to set fire to the sea with oil to stop any German landing. This rumour was false.

(485) Although America did not enter the war until 1941, it was hardly neutral. Roosevelt gave military aid to Britain and the Americans assisted the British in the Atlantic convoys.

(486) The importance and might of Allied air power was illustrated just after D-Day when Panzer Group West had its headquarters attacked by Allied planes just as it was preparing to launch a counter-attack against the troops that had landed in Normandy. Panzer Group West lost many of its officers and vehicles in the air attack.

(487) Men on U-boats had to work eight hour shifts. If you served on a U-boat you didn't get your own bed either. You

would have to share a bunk on a shift system with someone else. This meant that when you went to bed you were using a dirty pillow and linen that someone else had been asleep in.

(488) The Chindits were a special forces group with Fourteenth Army in Burma. The Chindits were led by the tough and eccentric Major General Orde Charles Wingate. Wingate was an adventurer and guerilla warfare expert. The Chindits were dropped behind Japanese lines to destroy communications and supplies and generally make a nuisance of themselves. The second Chindit operation was the largest airborne operation of the war and dropped 30,000 men behind Japanese lines.

(489) Orde Wingate died in a plane crash in India in 1944. Winston Churchill was very sad about this because Wingate was something of a golden boy to Churchill. Churchill said that Wingate was like Lawrence of Arabia.

(490) Field Marshal Alan Brooke said in his diaries that he hardly got any sleep during the war because Winston Churchill was always having impromptu conferences at 3 in the morning or other equally eccentric hours.

(491) Hitler also kept what you might call bohemian hours for most of the war. Hitler would stay up late watching films and having conferences and then sleep until noon.

(492) Montgomery's 21st Army Group was sent to northern Germany near the end of the war in case the Red Army got any ideas about moving into Denmark.

(493) The soft drink Fanta was created in 1940 by Coca-Cola Deutschland under the leadership of German businessman Max Keith. The creation of the drink was a result of trade sanctions on Nazi Germany. Fanta was created as an alternative to (the unavailable) coca-cola.

(494) The Type VII C U-boat was the most common German

submarine during the war. 568 of these were built.

(495) Hitler was Austrian but became a staunch German patriot. He served in World War I as a runner between trenches and also experienced life as an impoverished and failed artist. Hitler was left with a deep and enduring bitterness when Germany lost the war and - a bigot and racist - he also developed a hatred of Jewish people who he scapegoated for Germany's problems. If Hitler had been a successful artist (as opposed to a penniless hack painter) then history might have been completely different.

(496) When the diaries of Field Marshal Alan Brooke, the head of the British Army and the most important British military figure of the war, were first published they had to be censored because of Brooke's blunt assessment of other personalities. Brooke's diaries revealed that he thought General Marshall (his American opposite number) and Field Marshal Alexander (Allied Commander of the Mediterranean) were both of below average intelligence. Brooke's diaries also criticised Winston Churchill for coming up with a number of crackpot military schemes that Brooke said he had to quash.

(497) A surfaced U-boat could travel at speeds of up to 17.7 knots.

(498) Himmler, who set up The Abnenerbe Institut (National Heritage Institute), dispatched archaeologists to search for evidence of Atlantis. Needless to say, evidence of this lost civilisation remained elusive.

(499) Right until his death in 1953, Stalin always believed that Hitler had escaped from the Berlin bunker.

(500) 60% of the Japanese soldiers who died in World War 2 died because of disease or malnutrition.

(501) The French were shrewd enough to destroy their submarines near the end of the Battle of France so they

wouldn't fall into German hands.

(502) A month after D-Day, the Allies had over 800,000 troops in France.

(503) The Red Army had two and a half million soldiers ready to attack Berlin at the end of the war.

(504) Over 30 million people died on the eastern front.

(505) More people died at Auschwitz than the entire war death toll of America and Britain.

(506) After the liberation of France by the Allies, 10,000 Nazi collaborators were executed by French resistance groups.

(507) The atomic bomb dropped on Hiroshima radiated heat 40 times that of the sun.

(508) 50% of the Gold the Nazis possessed during the war was shipped off to Swiss banks.

(509) Switzerland was neutral in the war. They traded heavily with Nazi Germany and closed the door to refugees. Switzerland was surrounded by Axis controlled countries.

(510) During World War 2, on Ramree Island off the coast of Burma, 1000 Japanese troops were driven into a swamp by the British. The Japanese soldiers were attacked by crocodiles and only 300 made it out alive.

(511) After the defeat at Stalingrad, the German people were asked to donate clothes and food for the soldiers in the east. This was the first sure sign the general public had that the war wasn't going all that swimmingly for Hitler.

(512) Hermann Göring said that he knew the war was lost when he saw that Allied bombers had long range fighter escorts.

(513) The most remarkable theory about Martin Bormann is that he was a Soviet agent in Berlin secretly sending information to Moscow. This would explain why Bormann hated the limelight and had a low profile. This conspiracy theory is not taken very seriously.

(514) When the war ended, Field Marshal Alan Brooke went to some celebrations in London and found that the public didn't have the faintest idea who he was. All of his important work had been done in conferences and behind the scenes.

(515) General Eisenhower was against use of the atomic bomb against Japan. Eisenhower believed that the use of these weapons would give America a bad reputation in the world.

(516) In 1945, the Toronto Daily Star reported that Hitler had escaped from his bunker and gone to Antarctica. The Nazis did actually stage expeditions to Antarctica to claim land and Admiral Dönitz spoke of the German submarine fleet building an invisible fortification in midst of the eternal ice during the Nuremberg Trials.

(517) Operation Valkyrie was the 20 July 1944 attempt by disgruntled German army officers to kill Hitler. Claus von Stauffenberg was the main figure in this and took a briefcase bomb into one of Hitler's conferences at his Wolf's Lair headquarters. Stauffenberg then left before the explosion and began telling his conspirators to start arresting the Nazi groups like the Gestapo. However, Hitler was saved by the fact there was a heavy oak table between him and the bomb. Goebbels quickly reported that Hitler was alive and the conspirators (who had assumed Hitler was dead) lost heart and didn't go through their plan to seize control of Germany. 7000 people were arrested in connection with the plot and nearly 5,000 were executed.

(518) Claus von Stauffenberg and the plotters were not motivated by any great moral light or decency. Many of them

were linked to war crimes on the eastern front and Stauffenberg didn't disagree with much of the Nazi system. The main motivation of these men was the fact that Germany was losing the war.

(519) Rommel was implicated in the plot to kill Hitler. While not directly involved he was sympathetic to the assassination plot and did listen to some of the plotters. After D-Day, Rommel was injured when his car was attacked by Allied planes. Hitler learned that Rommel was vaguely connected to the plotters and Rommel was given the option of taking a cyanide pill in return for his family's safety (it was a common Nazi tactic to keep people in line by threatening their family). Rommel took the suicide option and was given a state funeral. The Nazi propaganda line was that Rommel died of injuries sustained during the fighter attack on his car.

(520) President Roosevelt had beaten polio in the 1920s but lost the use of his legs. He created a treatment centre for polio patients and later resumed his political career.

(521) Audie Murphy was one of the most decorated American soldiers of World War 2. He received every military combat award for valor available from the US Army. After the war, Murphy had a film career (even playing himself in one film) and appeared in a lot of westerns. He died in a plane crash in 1971.

(522) The Germans had limited artillery ammunition when the Allies landed on D-Day. Some German divisions ran out of artillery ammunition by noon.

(523) One thing that made the Axis forces invading the Soviet Union tricky for Germany to handle was that the Romanians and the Hungarians didn't get on very well. The Germans put the Italian Army between the Romanians and the Hungarians as a consequence.

(524) After the war, Manstein said that the Romanian troops

had been the best soldiers out of Germany's allies in the war.

(525) The Italian army was notoriously poor in World War 2. There are a number of theories for this. The main theory is that Italian soldiers (unlike German soldiers at the start of the conflict) never really believed in the war and so were loath to sell their lives cheaply. The Italian soldiers also had to make do with out of date weapons and equipment. Their training was also poor compared to that of German soldiers.

(526) The translation of Wehrmacht is Armed Force. Wehr stands for resistance, macht means to make.

(527) The British Army used 80 million Benzedrine Sulphate pills during the war.

(528) Stalin allowed Marshal Zhukov to take the final salute in the Soviet victory parade. The reason for this that Stalin couldn't ride a horse and didn't want to look stupid by falling off.

(529) Later in the war, the Red Army could mass 400 artillery pieces for every mile of front. That was devastating firepower.

(530) During the Battle of Hurtgen Forest, the American 15th Engineer Combat Battalion lifted 1,352 mines and disarmed 125 pillboxes in the early waves.

(531) The Battle of Hürtgen Forest was a fight for a wooded area on the Belgian-Germany border fought by Americans and Germans. It was a bloody and tough battle. The Germans lost but managed to hold up the Allied advance for six months in this specific area. 30,000 American soldiers were killed or wounded in this battle.

(532) The Sonderfahndungsliste G.B. (Special Search List Great Britain) was a Nazi list of all the people in Britain who were to be arrested in the event of a successful invasion of Great Britain by Germany. The list included many famous

names like EM Forster, HG Wells, Noël Coward, Virginia Woolf, Stephen Spender, JB Priestley, Paul Robeson, and Sigmund Freud.

(533) For some reason, the Nazis also intended to arrest Robert Baden-Powell - the elderly founder of the boy scout movement.

(534) Only 20% of Allied bomber crewmen managed to parachute to safety after their plane was hit.

(535) On 20 June, 1942, a Japanese submarine fired on Estevan Point lighthouse off Vancouver Island, British Columbia. This was the only Axis attack on Canadian soil.

(536) A private in the US 2nd Armoured Div found the Generalfeldmarschall's baton belonging to Albert Kesselring (who was a Generalfeldmarschall of the Luftwaffe and commander in chief of the Western and Italian fronts) in a castle and took it home after the war. In 2010, the baton sold at an auction for $731,600.

(537) Winston Churchill is credited with the phrase 'iron curtain' to describe Soviet dominated eastern Europe. However, Goebbels might have used this phrase first.

(538) Coffee was never rationed in Britain during the war because it wasn't a very popular drink at the time and so there was plenty to go around.

(539) The British codebreakers at Bletchley Park were reluctant to share any secrets with the Americans at first when the United States entered the war.

(540) After the Battle at Kursk, the Germans were reduced to fighting a mostly defensive war in the east.

(541) Hitler was furious when he heard that Operation Spring Awakening (the 1945 offensive in Hungary) had failed and

suggested that the SS Divisions involved should have their insignias removed. The Waffen SS officers were equally furious when they heard this and considered putting their insignias in a big pot and sending them to Berlin.

(542) Germany had 1250 of the ME262 jet fighters at one point but because Hitler insisted they become bombers only 50 were able to go into service. This was a big blunder.

(543) The Panzerfaust was a shoulder-type German antitank weapon. You can see many German soldiers and Hitler Youth carrying one of these in photos and films from the Battle of Berlin. The weapon had limited range but was very effective in stopping tanks. You had to be brave to use one because the best tactic was to get close to the tank you wanted to aim at.

(544) By the later stages of the war, the Panzerfaust could penetrate almost 8 inches of armour.

(545) The Red Army destroyed 25 German divisions in 12 days during part of Operation Bagration.

(546) Marshal Georgi Zhukov developed a taste for Coca-Cola after Eisenhower introduced the drink to him during the war.

(547) In early 1945, the 6th Panzer Army's commander Sepp Dietrich said "We call ourselves the 6th Panzer Army, because we've only got 6 Panzers left."

(548) During World War 2, the US Army Corps of Engineers covered the Lockheed Burbank Aircraft Plant in camouflage netting to make it safe from any potential Japanese attack.

(549) General Omar Bradley loathed snipers for the cruel way they would leave wounded men as live 'bait'. Bradley said he would turn a blind eye to any rough treatment captured German snipers got.

(550) Old Trafford, the home of Manchester United, was

bombed during the war.

(551) It was said that during World War 2, Japanese soldiers hated using flamethrowers because they had an inherent fear of fire.

(552) After Italy was knocked out of the war, the Germans took 100,000 Italian Carcano rifles back to Germany to give to the Volksstum (the newly created Nazi Home Guard).

(553) The French fashion designer Coco Chanel was sympathetic to the German cause and worked for Nazi intelligence during the war.

(554) There were twenty-seven prisoner of war camps in Canada during the war. A lot of German prisoners thought Canada was so nice they asked to stay there permanently when the war was over.

(555) The British Army had a manpower problem late in 1944 and was low on infantry replacements. The solution was to divert some naval and air force personnel into the army. This is what Nazi Germany did too when it struggled to find enough soldiers.

(556) The United States executed about 140 of its own soldiers during the war. This punishment was mostly for murder and rape rather than desertion.

(557) The 3rd SS Panzer Division stranded in the Demyansk Pocket was often strafed by the Luftwaffe by mistake.

(558) The Nazi high circle clung to a false belief and hope that Britain and the United States would fall out and grow weary of their alliance.

(559) In the run up to D-Day, the Allies needed 25,000 special trains to move men, equipment, and ammunition to the starting point on the coast.

(560) Canadian bombing crews would sometimes throw milk bottles out over Germany because the whistling sound the bottles made was rather like a bomb falling and made anti-aircraft gunners on the ground twitchy and more liable to waste precious ammunition.

(561) The bocage country of Normandy was perfect for German snipers.

(562) British munitions factories kept going 24 hours a day.

(563) General Matthew Ridgeway, commander of the US 82nd Airborne Division, liked to have hand grenades on his jacket to show that he was still a soldier and not just an officer. His staff made him use deactivated hand grenades to stop any accidents from happening.

(564) Stalin was deeply unimpressed when he learned that the Western Allies were going to invade Italy. Stalin thought this would be a piddling sideshow and not the Second Front that he had been promised. The invasion of Italy did though tie down down around a million German soldiers and many Luftwaffe planes that otherwise could have been diverted to the east.

(565) Potatoes were not rationed in Britain during the war. Chip shops were still open but only at weekends.

(566) Desmond Llewelyn, who played Q in the James Bond films, was a prisoner of war at Colditz.

(567) The ration pack for American soldiers in the war would typically contain canned beans, packaged meats and vegetables, soluble fruit drinks, chewing gum, and cigarettes.

(568) By 1939, 90% of German children were in the Hitler Youth.

(569) The Hitler Youth dated back to 1926. It started as a German version of the British boy scout movement but became more militaristic. Hitler Youth children also were trained to be snoopers and sneaks who reported any anti-Nazi activity. The purpose of the Hitler Youth was essentially to ensure that the next generation of adults were loyal to Hitler and the Nazi Party.

(570) The Volkssturm was often drafting 12-year-old Hitler Youth members into its ranks by the end of the war.

(571) By 1944 there were around 30,0000 foreign soldiers in the Waffen SS.

(572) It is estimated that there were 22,000 civilian deaths in the Battle for Berlin.

(573) Germany had so little fuel near the end of the war that new aircraft were not flight tested. They were just sent straight to their Luftwaffe units.

(574) In his last days in the bunker, Hitler would wistfully study development plans and models for his home town of Linz in Austria. These plans would never happen now.

(575) The Luftwaffe lost about 50,000 aircraft in the war.

(576) The fighting in Stalingrad from August to November 1942 cost the VI and IV Panzer Armies 150,000 casualties.

(577) The United States supplied the Soviet Union with 6,430 planes, 3,734 tanks, and 104 ships and boats

(578) Hitler planned to rebuild Berlin into a new 'world' capital and rename it Germania. Germania was intended took like some magnificent city in ancient Rome.

(579) The British were short of military grade binoculars when they entered the war so they used secret agents to procure

German made ones through Swiss businesses.

(580) In the Far East, a team of 48 British snipers once killed 296 Japanese soldiers in two weeks.

(581) Food was rationed in America during the war. Roosevelt ended the rationing of coffee though in 1943.

(582) Britain supplied the Soviet Union with 5,800 planes, 4,292 tanks, and 12 minesweepers.

(583) In his December, 1941 war diary entries, Alan Brooke wrote that Winston Churchill wanted to send some British infantry divisions to fight with the Red Army against the Germans on the eastern front. Nothing came of this though (which was a relief to Brooke and the British infantry divisions in question).

(584) By the end of 1942, German soldiers in the east had clocked up 250,000 cases of frostbite.

(585) The German surrender seemed to make no difference to their Axis allies Japan. Japan just carried on fighting.

(586) At the end of the Battle for Iwo Jima, only 1% of the Japanese garrison was left alive.

(587) The Battle for Iwo Jima was important because the Americans needed the island to use as a bomber runway.

(588) General Marshall and General MacArthur wanted to use mustard gas against Japanese soldiers dug into underground fortifications on Pacific islands but Roosevelt would not permit this.

(589) 40% of German males born between 1920 and 1925 were dead or missing at the end of World War 2.

(590) Almost a third of German ships sunk in Europe were as

a result of mines laid by planes.

(591) The Soviet Union built twice as many tanks as Germany in 1943.

(592) After the German collapse, Mussolini tried to escape across the Swiss border in April 1945. Mussolini, his mistress Clara Petacci, and fascist leaders, were captured by Italian partisans. They were shot and then the bodies of Mussolini and Petacci were dumped on the Piazzale Loreta, a suburban square near the main railway station. This spot was chosen because fifteen partisans had been executed there in 1944. A crowd soon gathered and the bodies of Mussolini and his mistress were beaten and spat at. The bodies were then hung up on public display at a petrol station.

(593) When Hitler saw what had happened to Mussolini, it understandably strengthened his desire to not be captured alive and also have his body burned before anyone could get hold of it.

(594) There were causalities as a result of friendly fire during the London Blitz. Sometimes the shells that had fired up at German planes would come back down and cause damage.

(595) By the spring of 1944, the Allies had ten times as many aircraft in Italy as the Germans.

(596) After the war, some German generals said they were puzzled by the Allies invading Italy from the south and fighting their way up. They said the Allies should have just invaded from the top rather than the bottom.

(597) The Allied invasion of Sicily was not a total success because the Germans successfully evacuated 50,000 soldiers.

(598) 132,000 Italians were killed or captured during the Allied invasion of Sicily.

(599) The U-boat crews called their submarines iron coffins.

(600) The number of combinations in a German Enigma code machine was 1,252,962,387,456.

(601) The cracking of the Enigma code meant that for a good portion of the war the Allies could see secret messages sent out by all branches of the German military.

(602) The Allies had to be careful in the way that they used the Enigma information because they didn't want the Germans to know their codes had been cracked. The breaking of the code was vital in many battles - especially at sea. The Allies decoded over a million German navy signals and messages during the war.

(603) The cracking of the Enigma code was aided by Polish cryptographers escaping from Poland with a replica Enigma machine.

(604) Alan Turing created the world's first digital electric computer in order to decode German communications.

(605) When the Sixth Army surrendered at Stalingrad, 24 German generals went into Soviet captivity.

(606) Nazi propaganda tried to pretend that the Sixth Army hadn't surrendered at Stalingrad but had been wiped out heroically fighting to the last bullet. This propaganda was soon proved to be bogus when the Soviets paraded German prisoners from Stalingrad through Moscow.

(607) Lice infections broke out amongst the trapped German soldiers at Stalingrad because it was too cold for them to wash themselves.

(608) The trapped German soldiers at Stalingrad were reduced to eating watery soup and living on 200 grams of bread a day. Even this meagre ration was eventually cut.

(609) Soldiers in the North African desert had to put up with mosquitoes, sandstorms, freezing cold nights, and scorpions.

(610) Of all the Germans divisions destroyed between 1941 and 1944, 75% were destroyed in 1944 alone.

(611) In one single day at the Battle of Kursk, the Germans lost 586 tanks.

(612) The NKVD shot 13,000 Soviet soldiers at Stalingrad for cowardice and being drunk. 13,000 was equivalent to the strength of a Red Army division.

(613) Panzer Divisions had reconnaissance battalions which were designed as the eyes and ears of the division. These reconnaissance battalions were supposed to roam free on vehicles and report what was going on. However, when Germany began to run low on soldiers, these reconnaissance battalions just ended up static and fighting desperate battles like any other soldier.

(614) The Fourth Panzer Army was supposed to rescue the Sixth Army at Stalingrad but they couldn't get close enough to open up a corridor. The Red Army was too strong. By that stage though it was probably too late. The Sixth Army wasn't capable of a fighting retreat in the end.

(615) During the Battle of Stalingrad, Red Army snipers would shoot any Russian children they saw filling up German water bottles in exchange for food. The snipers considered these children to be traitors.

(616) The only recording of Hitler speaking in his normal voice (as opposed to ranting madly in speeches) was secretly taped by the Fins when Hitler met Carl Gustaf Emil Mannerheim, Commander-in-Chief of the Finnish Defence Forces, during a secret visit honoring Mannerheim's 75th birthday on 4 June 1942. The meeting took place in a train carriage in southern

Finland. Thor Damen, an engineer for the Finnish broadcasting company Yle, recorded the first 11 minutes of Hitler and Mannerheim's private conversation before SS guards noticed what he was doing and stopped him. The chilling thing about the recording is that Hitler's natural voice sounds so normal. In the conversation, Hitler does nearly all of the talking and rambles on and on about Soviet munitions production.

(617) The 101st Airborne Division, which performed so heroically during the Battle of the Bulge and other battles, was the focus of the excellent Steven Spielberg HBO miniseries Band of Brothers.

(618) Near the end of the war, Guderian wanted to evacuate German troops from Italy, Denmark, Sweden, and Courland to use against the Red Army offensive on the Oder. However, Hitler refused to allow this. Hitler hated evacuating troops from foreign territories because it merely reminded him that his Nazi Empire was shrinking fast.

(619) After Operation Bagration, 200,000 German troops were trapped in Courland. Guderian desperately wanted these troops evacuated but Hitler insisted they stayed where they were as a staging post for a future attack (this was a ludicrous fantasy on the part of Hitler). The end result was that 200,000 soldiers who could have been used to defend Berlin were now effectively sitting out the rest of the war. Stalin called the trapped Army Group Courland the 'largest prison camp in the world'.

(620) In August 1842, in an attempt to divert German soldiers from the eastern front and mitigate the fact that they hadn't opened a Second Front for Stalin, the Allies staged an amphibious attack on the French port of Dieppe. The raid was a failure and wiped out most of the 5,000 Canadian troops who spearheaded the attack. The attack's main flaw was that it lacked proper sea and air support. It taught the Allies a few important lessons they would remember for D-Day.

(621) When the captured Nazis were given IQ tests in preparation for the Nuremberg trials, Hjalmar Schacht came top. Schacht was the former German Minister of Economics. He was furious to be in the Nuremberg trials because he had been critical of Hitler and the Nazis and sent to a concentration camp. As a result of this, Hjalmar Schacht was let off by the Allies and set free.

(622) Hermann Göring was the third most intelligent of the captured Nazis at the Nuremberg trials according to the IQ tests.

(623) The person who recorded the lowest IQ of the captured Nazis at the Nuremberg trials was Julius Streicher. Streicher was the founder and publisher of the antisemitic Nazi newspaper Der Stürmer and was later a Gauleiter and politician. Julius Streicher was found to be one of the craziest Hitler fanatics at the trials. He kept trying to read out antisemitic quotes and expressed no regret for anything the Nazis had done.

(624) It was always assumed that General Douglas MacArthur would have a good chance of becoming President after the war. However, MacArthur's political career didn't quite go according to plan and - to the surprise of many - it was General Eisenhower who had a successful career in politics and ended up in the White House.

(625) When the Americans were 'island hopping' in the Pacific, they would sometimes find abandoned islands that the Japanese had left booby trapped.

(626) The aftermath of World War 2 saw eastern Europe and half of Germany become satellite states of the Soviet Union. The Cold War had begun.

(627) Germany was split into four occupied zones after the war. The United States, Britain, the Soviet Union, and France

all had a zone. Roosevelt didn't want to give France a zone but Churchill persuaded him this was a good idea.

(628) Germany soldiers in the latter stages of the war had a low opinion of the Luftwaffe but a high opinion of the navy. The German ships used to their guns to give the army welcome artillery support in the east.

(629) Hitler dismissed the threat of America before Roosevelt entered the war after Pearl Harbour. Hitler said Americans were only good at making iceboxes and fridges.

(630) Hitler was saved in the July the 20th bomb plot because the conference took place in a wooden hut. The usual conference room was concrete but it was undergoing some renovations that day and wasn't used. If the conference had taken place in a concrete room then Hitler would not have survived.

(631) As a result of the 20th of July plot bomb blast, 200 wooden splinters had to be removed from Hitler's body.

(632) Among the substances that Theodor Morell gave Hitler by means of drops, injections, pills, or other methods, are cocaine, testosterone, barbiturates, opiates, methamphetamine, and bromide.

(633) It has been speculated that Hitler's poor health (and perhaps too his grim and tragic outlook on the world) was a result of contracting syphilis as a young man. In his early writings, Hitler was obsessed with syphilis and called it a Jewish disease.

(634) Japanese soldiers in the jungle had a tactic of following an advance with a wide flanking arc on either side. It was Australian troops who first noticed this and amended their tactics accordingly to deal with it.

(635) General Eisenhower was later the first American

President to travel in a helicopter.

(636) The British Fourteenth Army in Burma had Gurkha units. Gurkhas are soldiers native to the Indian subcontinent. They are feared soldiers known for their bravery and ferocity. The Gurkhas carry an 18 inch curved sword known as a kukri. Gurkhas still serve in the British Army to this day.

(637) Germany essentially lost the war in the west as soon as the Allies got a foothold in Normandy. Once the Allies were ashore and ready to move there was no way for the German armed forces to stop them. Hitler's only chance was to stop an invasion or the beaches or at sea.

(638) Over three million Soviet prisoners of war died in German camps.

(639) The German plan for the civilian population of Stalingrad and Leningrad was simply to let everyone starve to death.

(640) Volksgrenadier Divisions were introduced to the German Army in 1944. Himmler is usually credited with the concept. Volksgrenadier Divisions were infantry divisions built around divisions that had largely destroyed. Men from the Luftwaffe and Kriegsmarine were used to pad these new divisions out.

(641) German generals generally had a low opinion of the Volksgrenadier Divisions because the men in them tended to lack experience of combat and hadn't recieved much training. Some of these divisions did perform well though. The paucity of manpower in Germany by 1944 was illustrated by the fact that a number of Volksgrenadier Divisions were used in the Battle of the Bulge.

(642) The Germans called Sherman tanks 'Tommy-cookers' when they first encountered them because the tanks seemed to catch fire a lot.

(643) Winston Churchill used to paint to relax during the war. Eisenhower got his love of painting from Churchill.

(644) Hitler suffered from halitosis.

(645) Phosphorus ammunition was used on the eastern front by the Soviets but as a smoke round. The use of this ammunition is controversial.

(646) Himmler tried to recruit a 'Russian army of Liberation' made up of Soviets POWs. A Russian volunteer division that did fight with the Germans against the Red Army was so ineffective the Germans withdrew it from the line and took the division's weapons away.

(647) Hitler's secretaries in the bunker had regular pistol practice in case they would have to fight off the Red Army. The women became very proficient sharpshooters.

(648) Near the end of the war, the Nazis tried to create an underground resistance movement called the Werewolves to fight the Red army. This partisan movement never really got off the ground. Apart from a few assassinations they didn't do much.

(649) The Panther tank was popular with its German crews because it had good armour and a powerful gun. It was though prone to breakdowns.

(650) The German battleship Prinz Eugen ended up being stuck in Denmark because of lack of fuel. It was handed over to the Americans when the war ended and destroyed in a 1946 atom bomb test.

(651) The first shots in World War 2 when it comes to Europe are said to have been a German battleship opening fire on a Polish garrison in the Bay of Danzig.

(652) After the Nazi-Soviet pact, the two countries carved up Poland. Both countries were equally ruthless and wicked in their orgies of murder and detention.

(653) A million Poles were sent to Siberia after the Nazi-Soviet Pact.

(654) On New Year's Day in 1945, the Luftwaffe attacked Allied airfields and destroyed 400 planes. However, the Luftwaffe lost 270 planes and 201 pilots in the attack. Replacing 400 planes was easy for the Allies but losing 270 planes was a disaster for Germany. The loss of these planes effectively finished off the Luftwaffe as an effective fighting force.

(655) The American hand grenade was, for obvious reasons, nicknamed the pineapple.

(656) An American Admiral in World War 2 once bugged a British military delegation in Washington so he could listen in on their private conversations.

(657) Things were so quiet on the western front just before the Battle of the Bulge that Montgomery asked Eisenhower if he could have the weekend off and go home to England.

(658) General Patton believed in reincarnation. He felt that he had fought great battles in Europe in past lives.

(659) The Germans started to run out of tungsten late in the war. This meant they couldn't produce much armour-piercing ammunition.

(660) In 1944, the Germans lost 70 ships in the eastern Baltic.

(661) German generals on the eastern front had a trick where their front line was a skeleton force that could be evacuated at the last minute. This meant that the Red Army's opening artillery barrage would fall on empty positions.

(662) Hitler never visited wounded German soldiers during the war.

(663) Secret Soviet orders were issued to prepare a rearguard defence of Moscow in case the Germans broke through.

(664) Britain's Bomber Command had 55,573 killed out of a total of 125,000 aircrew.

(665) Bomber Command flew 364,514 operational sorties in the war.

(666) Britain manufactured over two million rifles between 1939 and 1944.

(667) At the end of the war there were around 19,000 American soldiers who had deserted in France and Germany.

(668) In 1946 the British government offered leniency for British World War 2 deserters still at large in Europe and a large number immediately gave themselves up.

(669) Air force personnel accounted for 27% of American military manpower in the war.

(670) The US Air Force had over 300 airfields in Europe by 1944.

(671) When they reached Berlin, the Americans found that 80% of the industrial machinery in the city had already been stripped and taken away by the Red Army.

(672) Hitler had 20,000 criminals taken from German prisons in 1942 to be executed by the SS.

(673) Concentration camp inmates were involved in constructing the V-2 rockets. The conditions for these forced labourers was grim. More people died making V-2 rockets

than were killed by them.

(674) The British Second Army (which was part of Montgomery's 21st Army Group) built 677 bridges in Europe after D-Day.

(675) The British Second Army captured 700,000 prisoners from D-Day to the end of the war.

(676) The American portable anti-tank rocket weapon was the Bazooka. The Germans and Japanese both used captured Bazookas to try and engineer similar weapons. The Bazooka took its name from a musical instrument invented by comedian Bob Burns.

(677) The British Army made 95,000 wireless sets during the war.

(678) In 1966, Marshal Zhukov gave an interview to Russian television in which he said that if Germany had attacked Moscow sooner the Red Army wouldn't have been able to stop them. This was contrary to Soviet propaganda so the government buried the interview and prevented it from being shown.

(679) In Russia, World War 2 is known as the Great Patriotic War. The Nazi-Soviet Pact tends to be glossed over or ignored. When Ukraine became independent from the (defunct) Soviet Union, it brought in a law to drop the term Great Patriotic War and replace it with Second World War.

(680) Believe it or not, Hitler was said to be a big fan of Laurel & Hardy.

(681) Thirteen million British houses were damaged by bombs in World War 2. However, only 200,000 of these were completely destroyed or damaged beyond repair.

(682) Hitler had a team of young women who had to test his

food to make sure it hadn't been poisoned. If the women ate the food and showed no effects for an hour the food was deemed safe and served to Hitler.

(683) Hitler's diet mostly consisted of rice, pasta, and vegetables.

(684) A German soldier who was present at one of Hitler's meals later wrote that the dictator had terrible table manners. The soldier said that Hitler ate rapidly and kept picking his nose.

(685) Task Force Baum was a battlegroup created by General Patton to go 50 miles behind German lines in march 1945 and try to liberate the POWs in camp OFLAG XIII-B, near Hammelburg. The motivation of Patton is believed to have been the fact that his son in law was a prisoner at the camp. Patton therefore kept the rescue mission a secret from his superiors. The mission was failure and out of 300 men, only 32 made it back. The rest were killed or captured. The 57 tanks and vehicles allocated to Task Force Baum were all lost. Eisenhower was furious when he found about about this secret mission and had to reprimand Patton.

(686) The total strength of all combined British Commonwealth armies at the end of the war was nearly nine million men.

(687) Winston Churchill had a secret bunker codenamed Paddock which was forty foot below ground in north-west London. The bunker was completely bombproof and big enough for a staff of 200 to work and live there. This bunker is where Winston Churchill and the military chiefs would have gone if the Battle of Britain had been lost.

(688) Men in Volksgrendier Divisions were sometimes dismayed to see that they had been partly equipped with out of date French weapons that the Germans had acquired after the fall of France some years earlier.

(689) The largest amount of depth charges dropped on a solitary U-boat during the war was 678 dropped onto U-427 in April, 1945. However, the U-boat somehow managed to survive.

(690) According to various interviews and books, Hitler's favourite films were Lives of a Bengal Lancer, King Kong, and Metropolis.

(691) It has been claimed that Hitler was a fan of the Marx Brothers. This would be ironic as they were Jewish.

(692) Over half of Nazi Germany's armaments budget in 1941 went on the Luftwaffe and Kriegsmarine. This figure seems strange in hindsight given that they had just embarked on a ground invasion of the Soviet Union. It suggests that they grossly underestimated the strength of the Red Army.

(693) Hitler had such a sweet tooth that he would put sugar in a glass of wine.

(694) The 200,000 or so British soldiers rescued at Dunkirk were important because they became the backbone of the British forces sent to the Middle East.

(695) The Royal Navy built 722 major vessels during the war.

(696) In 2014, Ben Urwand wrote a book in which he claimed that Hollywood studios, in order to maintain their access to the Germany market in the 1930s, financed German weapons and even aborted a plan to make a film about Jewish mistreatment in Germany because the Nazis complained. It should be noted that other film historians have refuted Urwin's claims. They point out that many studio executives were Jewish themselves and actively involved in anti-Nazi groups.

(697) Adolf Hitler's eastern front headquarters for much of the

war was the Wolf's Lair (Wolfschanze). This was located near Rastenburg in East Prussia (now the town of Ketrzyn in Poland). Hitler spent more time at the Wolf's Lair than anywhere else. It was built just before Operation Barbarossa.

(698) The Wolf's Lair was in a heavily wooded area and covered in camouflage. There were about 2000 staff at the headquarters. It had eighty buildings and heavy bunkers. The Wolf's Lair was close to a series of lakes that served as a natural defence from any eastern attack. 50,000 mines were laid around the headquarters to ensure it was completely safe. The compound also had flak batteries in case of an air attack.

(699) The Wolf's Lair was abandoned by the Nazis in November 1944 because the Red Army were too close for comfort.

(700) Otto Kretschmer was the most successful U-boat captain in terms of Allied tonnage sunk. Kretschmer sank 273.043 tons. He was captured by the British in 1941 after his U-boat was scuttled.

(701) Otto Kretschmer sank 46 ships in his career as a U-boat captain.

(702) General Gunther Blumentritt wrote an article about Sealion (the Nazi invasion of Britain) after the war and said that the German staff didn't believe the operation was feasible. The main problem would have been supplying the invasion army and Blumentritt felt this would have been impossible with the dominance of the Royal Navy (who would simply have sunk as many German supply ships as possible). Blumentritt estimated that, after an initial landing, it would have taken two weeks to get the German Panzer Divisions to the south coast of England. By that stage the invasion might already have been repulsed.

(703) The actor Alec Guinness drove landing craft during the war.

(704) The first Japanese sniper rifle was developed in 1937. The Japanese military decided to have more snipers after experiencing Chinese snipers in action.

(705) The average age of a Japanese kamikaze pilot was 18 to 24. More mature and experienced pilots were not sacrificed because these men were too valuable as flight instructors.

(706) Rod Serling, the creator of the classic television show The Twilight Zone, was a paratrooper in World War 2 and fought in New Guinea before taking part in the invasion of the Philippines. He suffered bad shrapnel wounds from combat.

(707) There are estimated to have been 3,912 Japanese kamikaze pilots.

(708) Japanese kamikaze pilots sank 34 American Navy ships.

(709) Japanese kamikaze pilots are estimated to have killed nearly 5,000 American sailors.

(710) Japanese kamikaze pilots sometimes used to fly between American ships in the hope of making the ships fire on each other by mistake.

(711) The actor Lee Marvin was in the US Marine Corps during the war and was injured in battle fighting the Japanese

(712) The Japanese used weaponised fleas on China. Fleas infected with bubonic plague were dropped out of aircraft over select Chinese cities from 1940 to 1941.

(713) The Krummlauf Curved Rifle was a Nazi attempt to create a rifle that shoot around corners! This weapon was not a great success though.

(714) The fighting in the Warsaw Uprising lasted for 63 days.

(715) To quash the Warsaw Uprising, the Nazis sent in Oskar Dirlewanger's Dirlewanger Brigade. Dirlewanger and his men were violent sadists who relished any chance to kill. They shot 40,000 people and set fire to hospitals that still had patients inside.

(716) When the war was over, Oskar Dirlewanger was arrested in the French occupation zone of Germany. He died in custody. It is speculated that he was beaten to death by guards.

(717) More than 40,000 Russian civilians were killed during the Battle of Stalingrad.

(718) James Doohan, forever immortal as Scotty in Star Trek, fought at Normandy with the Canadian Army.

(719) The Japanese invented a plane for kamikaze missions called the Yokosuka MXY7 Ohka (Cherry Blossom). The plane was rather like a missile with wings.

(720) 1,900 kamikazes were deployed at the Battle of Okinawa.

(721) On D-Day, the Germans sent nineteen U-boats to attack the invasion fleet but the Royal Air Force quickly sank one of the U-boats and damaged five others. The U-boats had to abandon their attack and were effectively eliminated as a threat.

(722) The Panther tank had sloped armour to make it more resistant to damage.

(723) The P. 1000 Ratte (Rat) was a proposed new German super tank considered in 1942. The tank would have weighed 1,000 tons and required twenty men to operate it. In the end the design never got off the drawing board because such a large tank would have been too heavy for many bridges and too big to enter villages or travel on small roads.

(724) By the end of the war there were around 20,000 Poles serving in the Royal Air Force.

(725) After the liberation of Dachau concentration camp, American soldiers killed some of Waffen-SS soldiers and SS camp guards who had surrendered at the camp.

(726) Hitler couldn't drive and so always needed a chauffeur.

(727) Red Army soldiers looted 25,000 train carriages worth of goods in Berlin and had it sent back to the Soviet Union. Wristwatches and bicycles were among their favourite things to loot.

(728) In October 1940, Mussolini invaded Greece from Albania. He had assumed Greece would be easy pickings but his army was driven back into Albania by the Greeks. It was, to say the least, very humiliating for Mussolini.

(729) Mussolini hadn't bothered to tell Hitler about his invasion of Greece. Hitler was furious when he found out. The Germans had to intervene to help Italy and also prevent the British from occupying Greece first.

(730) Mussolini is believed to have invaded Greece in a fit of pique because he was angry that Hitler had annexed Romania without consulting Italy. Italy considered Romania to be part of their sphere of influence.

(731) The United States sent the Soviet Union 2,000 railway locomotives during the war.

(732) The Waffen SS made up 34% of all German soldiers killed in the war.

(733) In the aftermath of Kursk and German strife on the eastern front, one German infantry division was left with just 300 men.

(734) One of the reasons why Hitler grossly underestimated the strength of the Red Army and always got annoyed when he was told how many divisions the Soviets had, was that he seemed to presume that Red Army divisions only contained a few thousand men. As a consequence of this, Hitler (wrongly) believed that the Red Army's real strength was being grossly inflated by his generals.

(735) Before the war, Hitler was friends with a little German Jewish girl called Rosa Bernile Nienau. Hitler invited Rose and her mother to have dinner with him because he read that they shared a birthday. When the war started, the Nazis contacted Rosa's mother and told her never to contact Hitler again. Hitler didn't know they had done this.

(736) The Republic of Ireland refused to allow Britain use of its ports in the war - a decision that cost many Allied lives at sea. Winston Churchill could have just seized the ports if he'd wanted to but decided this would be too controversial.

(737) Believe it or not, there were Irish politicians who hated Britain so much that they didn't seem especially bothered by the thought of Hitler winning the war.

(738) Joachim von Ribbentrop was Foreign Minister of Nazi Germany from 1938 until 1945. He was the ambassador to Britain before the war and also played a key role in the Nazi-Soviet Pact. Ribbentrop was a businessman before the war and impressed Hitler because he seemed to have more knowledge of foreign countries than most Nazis. This didn't really turn out to be the case. Most of the Nazis thought that Ribbentrop was an idiot who didn't know much about anything.

(739) Nazi Germany eventually found itself at war with most of the world. This meant that there obviously wasn't much need for a foreign minister. As a consequence, Joachim von Ribbentrop found that his importance and influence with Hitler waned considerably. In the end he found it impossible to even get a meeting with Hitler.

(740) On the 16th of October 1946, Joachim von Ribbentrop became the first of those sentenced to death at Nuremberg to be hanged.

(741) Sweden arrested Allied agents during the war. They eased up on this when they deduced that Hitler wasn't going to be victorious.

(742) The American Red Cross had separate blood supplies for black and white soldiers so that white soldiers wouldn't be given blood from a black person. This is something that seems amazingly bizarre and racist today.

(743) Denmark refused to participate in the German request to deport Jews. As a consequence of this, most of the Jewish people in Denmark survived.

(744) Switzerland made huge profits from its trade with Nazi Germany but hardly gave any money to Jewish victims after the war.

(745) Large numbers of people in the Baltic States enlisted in the German Army because they hated Stalin and the Soviet Union so much.

(746) Stalin gave Marshal Zhukov some out of the way commands after the war because he feared that Zhukov's popularity and war hero status might make him a political threat.

(747) Japan lost over 200,000 men occupying China from 1941 to 1945. This was almost as many Japanese soldiers as the British killed in the war.

(748) The American chiefs of staff and Roosevelt had a policy called Germany First. As the name suggests, this meant that the priority for the United States was to defeat Hitler first and then turn their full attention to Japan. The division of

resources agreed in 1943 was that 70% of American military power would fight Germany and 30% would be directed against Japan in the Pacific.

(749) Admiral Nimitz and General Douglas MacArthur did not agree on Pacific strategy and ran parallel but distinct campaigns. Nimitz wanted to take a more direct route to Japan than MacArthur.

(750) By the end of the war, the United States had a larger navy than all the other combatants combined.

(751) Stalin was known as the Man of Steel in the Soviet Union. The Allies called him Uncle Joe.

(752) In a poll at the end of the war, Americans voted MacArthur the best general. MacArthur wasn't much liked by the military establishment but the public loved him.

(753) Denmark provided 10% of Germany's food during the war.

(754) By late 1944, foreign slave labour made up 20% of Nazi Germany's workforce.

(755) One of the masterstrokes of Operation Bagration was that the Red Army put dummy installations and tanks in north Ukraine to make the Germans think the offensive was going to be launched from there.

(756) The British Army used the Lee Enfield bolt rifle in the war. This was a very reliable weapon.

(757) The British submachine gun was the Sten. The American submachine gun was the .45 Thompson.

(758) The British used the Bren light-machine gun. This is quite an iconic weapon.

(759) The German MP38 and MP40 machine-pistols were excellent weapons for the time.

(760) The British Cromwell and Churchill tanks were no match for the Panthers and Tigers.

(761) When the Soviets launched Operation Bagration, the Germans were defending a front that was 1,400 miles long. This was an impossible length of front to defend - especially against an army that had many more men, guns, and tanks.

(762) Of the 400,000 men the Red Army trained to crew tanks, over 300,000 of them died in the war.

(763) Winston Churchill would sarcastically refer to Hitler as Corporal Hitler. This was, as we have noted, the highest rank Hitler attained in his military career.

(764) The German Army abandoned Paris without a fight after the Allies moved inland. Many German officers were very fond of Paris and had no stomach for destroying the city in a futile last stand against the Allies.

(765) American submarines were responsible for over one half of Japanese shipping losses.

(766) Japanese anti-submarine and radar technology was primitive compared to the Allies.

(767) Japan and Germany were similar in that they could only win a very short war. Once they found themselves in a long battle of attrition against a coalition that had a larger industrial base their hopes of victory vanished.

(768) The Japanese made a big strategic error by not building enough escort or supply ships.

(769) The Atlantic Wall was a series of fortifications the Germans built around the French and Scandinavian coast to

stop any invasion. It consisted of pillboxes, forts, tank traps, and various obstacles. The fortifications were never really completed though. Rommel was unimpressed by the Atlantic Wall when he arrived in France before D-Day.

(770) Hitler spent a lot of time in Obersalzberg - a mountain retreat area above the town of Berchtesgaden in the Bavarian Alps. This was where Hitler wrote Mein Kampf. Hitler bought a small house in the area in the 1920s and when the Nazis assumed power they created a huge complex of Nazi buildings there. All the top Nazis naturally got themselves a house in Obersalzberg so they could be close to the leader.

(771) The Eagle's nest was built for Hitler at Obersalzberg by Martin Bormann. This retreat was 6,000 feet up and built on the inside of a mountain. Hitler made some of his biggest decisions at the Eagle's Nest. The Alpine mountain complex of Blofeld in the James Bond film On Her Majesty's Secret Service was based on the Eagle's Nest.

(772) The British bombed the Nazi Obersalzberg complex on 25 April 1945 because of an Allied fear that the mountains might be used by the Germans to fight a last stand. The buildings that had housed Hitler and the Nazis were then looted by locals and Allied soldiers.

(773) When the Germans were given control of Obersalzberg again after the war they had to agree to destroy any Nazi buildings that were still standing. The American Army did actually keep hold of a few of these Nazi buildings and houses at Obersalzberg so that their soldiers could use them for recreation.

(774) Franz Halder, the OKH chief of staff, said that Hitler would 'fly into an insane rage' when anyone tried to present him with figures that showed the strength of the Red Army.

(775) Generalfeldmarschall Paul von Kleist said after the war that the Germans could have taken Stalingrad without a fight

if Hitler hadn't diverted the Fourth Panzer Army from Stalingrad to the Don. By the time the Fourth Army was turned north again it was too late.

(776) Sixty German cities suffered major bomb damage during the war.

(777) Albert Speer said after the war that, in his view, the Allied bombing of Germany did not damage morale or destroy the munitions industry.

(778) Albert Speer estimated that the Allied bombing campaign kept 10,000 anti-aircraft guns in Germany that might otherwise have been sent to the eastern front.

(779) When the fog cleared during the Battle of the Bulge, the Allied planes flew 15,000 sorties in four days.

(780) Reinhard Heydrich was one of the most brutal Nazis. He was a protege of Himmler and a leading figure in the genocide of the Jews. Heydrich also created the Einsatzgruppen death squads who were responsible for numerous atrocities in the east.

(781) Reinhard Heydrich was appointed Reich-Protector of Bohemia and Moravia and became infamous for his brutal leadership. He sent thousands of people to concentration camps and was known as the Hangman and the Butcher of Prague.

(782) On the 27th of May, 1942, four Czech resistance fighters who had been trained in Britain, ambushed the car Heydrich was in and managed to throw a hand grenade. Heydrich was badly injured and died seven days later.

(783) In retaliation for the death of Heydrich, the Germans killed all the men and boys over fifteen in the village of Lidice. The women were sent to concentration camps and the village was then burnt to the ground.

(784) Reinhard Heydrich was ruthlessly ambitious and also good looking and blond. Many believe that he was the most likely successor to Hitler before his death.

(785) Hitler was furious at the death of Heydrich. He thought Heydrich had been stupid for always going around in an open top car and making himself such a target. Hitler was always fearful of an assassination attempt and would constantly change his schedule at the last minute so that one could never quite be sure where he was. This routine saved Hitler's life on more than one occasion.

(786) Of the 7,000 guards who worked at Auschwitz, only 400 were ever captured and put on trial for their crimes.

(787) The Japanese Army became infamous for atrocities in World War 2. They raped, beheaded, murdered children, used people for bayonet practice, and killed patients in hospitals. If a Japanese submarine sank a ship they would often shoot at lifeboats and torture any survivors they picked up.

(788) General Patton had ivory handed revolvers. He also liked a polished steel helmet and riding boots.

(789) The fact that Stalingrad bore Stalin's name was clearly a factor in why Hitler and Stalin became obsessed with the city.

(790) Germany lost 29 U-boats in three months at the start of 1944.

(791) Despite the U-boats, the size of the British merchant fleet stayed more or less the same during the war. The British were able to replace lost ships.

(792) Rommel said before D-Day that if an Allied invasion of France wasn't stopped inside 48 hours then Germany would have lost the war in the west. He was proved to be completely right.

(793) There were 59 German Divisions in the west at the time of D-Day. While this sounds impressive on paper, only 10 of those divisions were armoured tank divisions.

(794) The Allied soldiers taking part in D-Day had an anti-gas chemical sprinkled onto their uniforms in case of a German gas attack. This anti-gas chemical was foul and made many soldiers vomit.

(795) The Allies timed D-Day for low-tide so that they would be able to see the beach obstacles.

(796) The average age of the American soldiers who stormed Omaha Beach on D-Day was 20.

(797) American Rangers had to scale cliffs to take out a German gun battery on D-Day.

(798) The Germans took too long to get their Panzer Divisions to the coast after the Normandy landings. The German tanks were fed ineffectively into the battle piecemeal rather than deployed as an effective concentrated force.

(799) Generalfeldmarschall Gerd von Rundstedt wanted to give up the south of France and the coast after D-Day and lure the Allies into a huge tank battle around Paris. Hitler disagreed with this strategy so it never went ahead.

(800) The Wolf's Lair was the size of 21 football pitches.

(801) The Wolf's Lair had a sauna and private cinema.

(802) It was only discovered after the war that Germany had cracked the British convoy codes for shipping.

(803) When the Germans began to find Operation Barborossa heavy going, Rundstedt proposed that the Germans should go right back to their original starting point and forget all about

trying to occupy the Soviet Union. Rundstedt felt that the German Army should be kept intact and strong to protect Germany from an eastern invasion. He was completely right about all of this but there was zero chance of Hitler listening to him.

(804) When the Allied troops reached Germany, cases of venereal disease skyrocketed because of their encounters with German prostitutes.

(805) In the eleven months following June 1944, the German Army lost over three million rifles.

(806) The capture of Budapest cost the Red Army 80,000 dead and 250,000 injured.

(807) American and British bombers dropped strips of foil to try and confuse German radar.

(808) The German commander in Budapest wanted to abandon the city without a fight. Needless to say, Hitler insisted on a futile last stand.

(809) Stalin was desperate to get Berlin before the Allies because of pride but also the Kaiser Wilhelm Institute for Physics. This was the German atomic research facility and Stalin wanted the Red Army to get there first. The Soviet Union was behind the Americans and British when it came to atomic research.

(810) Adolf Hitler's father was called Alois Schicklgruber. Schicklgruber changed his name to Hitler.

(811) Rationing was quite severe in France during the war because a third of produce in France was sent to Nazi Germany. The French had to drink chicory instead of coffee and there were no potatoes. Bread was highly rationed too.

(812) The Bell (Die Glocke) was an alleged Nazi weapon found

in an SS base after the war. It was described a being a metal bell shaped object 15 feet high with two counter-rotating cylinders. There was a theory that this was a super weapon capable of 'jellyfying' anyone who got close. The more plausible theory is that it was merely the remains of a cooling tower.

(813) The German writer Norman Ohler, in his book about drug use in Nazi Germany, said that Dr Gerhard Orzechowski, the head pharmacologist of the naval supreme command on the Baltic, worked on a cocaine chewing gum for soldiers. The Nazis were always looking for a way to 'stimulate' their soldiers and give them an edge on the battlefield.

(814) Joseph Goebbels and his wife committed suicide in Hitler's bunker near the end of the war but only after killing their six children with cyanide capsules. The children were innocent of any Nazi crimes and had their whole lives ahead of them. Goebbels and his wife were so mentally ill with Nazism that they couldn't bear the thought of their children living in a world with no Adolf Hitler.

(815) 4% of the pre-war Japanese population were killed in World War 2.

(816) American ships in the Pacific had ice cream making facilities.

(817) The US Army Airborne Department experimented with the idea of dropping paratroopers out of gliders.

(818) The Americans dropped leaflets before they flattened Japanese cities with bombs. The leaflets urged the Japanese people to flee the cities and revolt against their government.

(819) Hitler's Wolf's Lair headquarters had two airports.

(820) It took until 1955 to make the area around the Wolf's Lair safe from mines.

(821) The German Panther tanks had an accurate and powerful 75mm cannon.

(822) Red Army soldiers had much lower cases of trench foot that the Germans. It is speculated that this is because Soviet soldiers wrapped their feet in linen bandages rather than use socks.

(823) The doors at Hitler's Reich Chancellery were made as big as possible so that guests would feel small and insignificant.

(824) The Soviets prepared for their attack on Berlin by studying models of the city.

(825) Eva Braun refused to leave the bunker near the end of the war and stayed at Hitler's side. They got married before their suicides.

(826) Some women in Berlin at the end of the war said that the first Soviet soldiers they met were kind and polite. The second wave of Soviet soldiers though only had raping and looting on their mind. It seems the first wave of soldiers were the more professional branch of the Red army.

(827) Hitler was understandably paranoid after the bomb plot and any generals who visited him thereafter were searched thoroughly by SS guards before a conference.

(828) Eva Braun killed herself by cyanide. Hitler shot himself in the right temple.

(829) The Wolf's Lair had a vegetable garden and two greenhouses so that Hitler could enjoy fresh food when he was there.

(830) The Simon Wiesenthal Center found documents which suggested at least 12,000 Nazis escaped to Argentina after the

war.

(831) During the siege of Leningrad, people ate glue made from animal bones because they were so hungry.

(832) Hitler, who was Austrian, only became a German citizen in 1932.

(833) The secretary of Joseph Goebbels broke a long silence and gave an interview at the age of 105. She said she had no idea about the extermination of the Jews because this was kept a secret from the German people. Her claim was taken with a grain of salt.

(834) A red telephone that Hitler used at the Wolf's Lair later sold at an auction for $243,000.

(835) Hermann Göring like to design his own uniforms and they became increasingly kitsch and silly as the war progressed. One German general said that Göring looked more like a man going to a costume party than a military officer.

(836) On September the 2nd, 1945, General Douglas MacArthur presided over the Japanese surrender on board the USS Missouri.

(837) Bernard Law Montgomery took over command of the British Eight Army in North Africa before he was authorised to do so and then axed all of the army's existing strategic plans without even reading them.

(838) Major-General Percy Hobart is not very well known today but during the war he was an innovator in the field of armoured warfare. Hobart's ideas led to the design of amphibious vehicles that were used to tackle obstacles in the D-Day landings.

(839) The Nazis developed a helicopter called the Flettner Fl 282 by the end of the war but the proposed fleet of helicopters

never went production because fuel and resources were too scarce by that stage.

(840) The Luftwaffe bombing population centres during the Battle of Britain was a strategic mistake. The effect of raids on Britain would have been much more militarily damaging if the Luftwaffe had directed all of their resources on bombing airfields, planes, and munitions installations.

(841) The Vichy French defenders of Madagascar held out for six months when the British invaded. The British were worried that Madagascar might become a supply base for the Japanese.

(842) An Indian Legion fought for the Germans in World War 2. This was made up of captured Indian soldiers who wanted India to be independent from Britain. The Indian Legion never amounted to that many men though.

(843) Late in the war, the Luftwaffe tried to use Me-109 fighters to destroy the tails of Allied bombers with its propeller. Use of these tactics downed seventeen Allied bombers on April the 7th, 1945. This however came at the large cost of 120 Luftwaffe pilots.

(844) Operation Tannenbaum was the codename for the German invasion of Switzerland. In 1940 a plan for 400,000 German and Italian troops to invade Switzerland was drawn up but this invasion never went ahead. The Swiss planned to fight a mountain guerrilla war should the Nazis invade. It is speculated that the Nazis didn't invade Switzerland in the end because they relied on the Swiss banking system and business contacts in the country.

(845) Foreign labour workers in Nazi Germany were not allowed to use shelters and subway stations during Allied air raids.

(846) The Type 5 Chi-Ri was a 37 ton Japanese tank intended

to give the Japanese the upper hand in tank battles with the Americans. However, only one prototype was made and the tank never went into production.

(847) When the Germans invaded France, Winston Churchill proposed a political union between France and Britain whereby the two countries worked under a single government and single military command. The French rejected this proposal.

(848) Lord Craigavon, the Prime Minister of Northern Island, asked Winston Churchill to send troops into the Republic of Ireland and topple the government so that Britain could use Irish ports in the war. Plans for such an operation were worked out but they were never carried through.

(849) The Nazis seriously considered an invasion of Northern Ireland with the help of their contacts in the IRA.

(850) A plan by US Secretary of the Treasury Henry Morgenthau in 1944 called for the defeated Germany to be turned into a primitive pastoral state shorn of heavy industry. Winston Churchill hated this plan because the west needed a strong and friendly Germany after the war as a barrier between the west and the Soviet Union.

(851) The Red Army had women in their anti-aircraft regiments at the Battle of Stalingrad. Many of these women had to take part in the ground fighting when the situation got desperate.

(852) The trapped Sixth Army at Stalingrad required 800 tons of supplies a day to remain fed and operational. On Overage, the Luftwaffe only managed to drop 94 tons a day.

(853) From 1941 onwards, the Red Army was responsible for 95% of Germany's military casualties in the war.

(854) 75,000 of the Germans who surrendered at Stalingrad

were dead within three months.

(855) Before the Battle of Kursk, the Germans estimated that the Soviets had 1,500 tanks to bring to bear. The real number was 3,000.

(856) Vasily Zaytsev was one of the most famous Red Army snipers in the war. Some claims have his kill count as high as 3000. Zaytsev actually set up a makeshift sniper training school in the rubble of Stalingrad during the battle.

(857) Ferdinand Porsche designed the Volkswagen Beetle after input by Hitler. Hitler wanted a German 'people's car'. Porsche spent some time in jail after the war because of his strong links to the Nazis.

(858) The Sturmtiger was a German tank built using the chassis of a Tiger tank. The tank was equipped with a powerful rocket launcher and was designed primarily for urban warfare. However, not many of these tanks were made and it didn't play a significant role in the war.

(859) The German Chief of the Army General Staff, Kurt Zeitzler, felt so guilty at the Sixth Army being trapped in Stalingrad that he only ate very basic rations as a means of solidarity with the starving soldiers hundreds of miles away. When he lost a large amount of weight, Hitler told him to stop being stupid and start eating again.

(860) When Charles de Gaulle visited Moscow after the war, he said it had been a remarkable feat by the Germans to get to the outskirts of the city in their invasion.

(861) On June 3rd, 1942, Japanese forces invaded and occupied Attu and Kiska - two islands that were part of Alaska.

(862) The capture of Moscow would have been a disaster for the Red Army because it was a huge railway hub. The Germans would have controlled vital rail routes the Soviet relied on to

move supplies and factories.

(863) In 1941, the Soviet Union had a population of nearly 200 million people. Germany had around 70 million people.

(864) The daily casualty rates for the Normandy campaign were more brutal than the Somme, Verdun & Passchendaele.

(865) The RAF bombed the invasion barges the Germans intended to use for Sealion quite extensively. This may have been a factor in the invasion not going ahead. Many of the barges were moored in Holland.

(866) During the siege of Leningrad, the Germans trained their guns on Lake Lagoda so that any supply ship trying to bring in food would be sunk.

(867) Japan built gigantic battleships in order to (so they hoped) negate any numerical inferiority they might encounter at war with the United States. The Yamato displaced (when loaded) 72,800 tonnes and her sister ship Musashi was equally huge. These are two of the largest battleships ever built. Both of these ships were sunk near the end of the war.

(868) After the war had ended, Alan Brooke said that if Hitler had invaded France in 1939 there would have been no way to defend Britain. By 1940, Britain had created 20 more Royal Air Force Squadrons and was in a much better position to defend itself.

(869) The Luftwaffe dropped gigantic magnetic naval mines on Leningrad.

(870) The Messerschmitt Me 163 was a rocket powered fighter built by the Germans. Around 300 were produced and its performance in combat was disappointing. It downed 16 aircraft for the loss of 10.

(871) A V-2 rocket cost about the same to produce as six

fighter aircraft. Given the diversion of resources (including scientists and precious fuel) into rocket production for minimal effect, many believe that the Nazis would have been better off scrapping the rocket programme and just spending the money on the Luftwaffe.

(872) A lot of windows were destroyed in Leningrad so many of the civilians in the siege were not only starving but also frozen.

(873) Hitler's secretary said he used to refer to Winston Churchill as 'that whiskey guzzler'.

(874) The Japanese battlegroup responsible for the attack on Pearl Harbour had 65 ships and 353 aircraft.

(875) The teahouse on the Mooslahnerkopf hill was often frequented by Adolf Hitler when he was at his Berghof at Obersalzberg. Hitler's secretary said that he would always order apple pie and that he preferred cocoa to tea or coffee.

(876) The Japanese attack on Peal Harbour did not target navy repair yards or the submarine base. This was a strategic mistake.

(877) In 1940, a 3,000lb German bomb landed in a street in England and created such a large crater that a bus fell into the hole.

(878) The Germans dropped parachute flares on Leningrad when they bombed it at night in order to illuminate the target area.

(879) 40 million gas masks were issued in Britain during the war.

(880) Stalin encouraged competition between his two most famous generals (Konev and Zhukov) in the last stage of the war to speed up the capture of Berlin. Konev was so eager to

get to Berlin that at one point his armies crashed into the rear echelons of Zhukov's armies - which created a lot of confusion.

(881) The 200,000-strong 1st Polish Army attacked Berlin with the Red Army. The Poles made up 10% of the forces attacking Berlin from the east.

(882) The Germans noticed on the eastern front that the Red Army would often attack in terrible weather. This was because the Soviets presumed their troops were less affected by the cold and difficult conditions and so would have an advantage.

(883) Volunteers from Francoist Spain formed a division known as the Blue Division/Spanish Volunteer Division to fight with the Germans on the eastern front. This division numbered around 45,000 men and fought well. Franco withdrew the Blue Division in 1943 when things started to turn sour for the Germans.

(884) Several hundred men from the Spanish Volunteer Division refused to go back to Spain and insisted on fighting on against the Red Army. Some of these Spanish volunteers even fought in the Battle of Berlin near the end of the war.

(885) The Soviet 203-mm howitzer B-4 as known as Stalin's sledgehammer. This gun could destroy pillboxes and level a house.

(886) Soviet troops carried cauldrons around with them which were used to cook and boil their food. A staple for Red Army soldiers in the war was kulesh. This was a soup made of millet.

(887) The Soviet Union used about 20,000 of the tanks sent to them by America and Britain. This made up about 16% of the tanks used by the Red Army in the war.

(888) Soviet factories produced 10,000 Katyusha rocket batteries between 1941 and 1945.

(889) A million people were made homeless by the Battle of Berlin.

(890) The Soviet 2nd Guards Tank Army lost 209 of its lend-lease Sherman tanks in the fighting for Berlin.

(891) Firstborn sons were exempt from kamikaze pilot recruitment so that their family name would continue.

(892) The beaches used for the Normandy landings stretched out for fifty miles in total.

(893) During the Winter War, the Fins actually got the better of the Soviet Air Force. The Soviets lost 190 planes while Finland only lost 47.

(894) The Germany Army suffered the amputation of nearly 15,000 limbs through frostbite on the eastern front by the end of 1941.

(896) Kamikaze pilots would have a special ceremony before their suicide missions. It was custom to drink sake at these 'farewell' ceremonies.

(897) Female Soviet pilots Lydia Litvyak and Yekaterina Budanova both downed over a dozen German planes.

(898) Stalin's Order No. 227 was known as the Not One Step Backward! directive. The directive stated that any Red Army soldiers who retreated without permission were to be shot.

(899) The last German POWs in the Soviet Union were not released until 1956 - over a decade since the end of the war.

(900) When the Germans invaded the Soviet Union, the Belorusian Military District's air force commander killed himself after viewing some of the Soviet airfields that the Luftwaffe had destroyed.

(901) Generalfeldmarschall Walther Model was another of the famous German generals who thought the Ardennes Offensive was a mistake. Model said that the operation only had a 10% chance of success.

(902) The 106th American Golden Lions Division was one of the biggest victims of the Battle of the Bulge. Because of a misunderstanding caused by a bad telephone line, its commander wrongly believed it had been ordered to stay where it was. Nearly 7,000 troops in the division surrendered to the Germans when their situation became hopeless.

(903) In his memoir, Guderian said the German plan for the attack on the Soviet Union envisaged a campaign of eight to ten weeks. Guderian thought this was ludicrously optimistic and so it proved to be.

(904) General Patton served in World War I and once walked around during shellfire chatting with a young officer he'd met. The young officer's name was Douglas MacArthur.

(905) The motto of the Fourteenth Army in Burma was 'God helps those who help themselves'.

(906) The teleprinter exchanges between the Sixth Army at Stalingrad and their Army Group reveal the gradual breakdown in communication and the exasperation of the trapped soldiers. During one exchange, General Schmidt (who was trapped in Stalingrad with the Sixth Army) simply signs off with this sarcastic and brief message - 'We suggest that the Luftwaffe should rather supply us with bread than drop a few and not always effective bombs before the Tatsinskaya front. I have nothing else.'

(907) Five German officers were executed on Hitler's orders for allowing the Allies to capture the bridge over the Rhine at Remegan.

(908) Britain made over nine million hand grenades in the

war.

(909) The ocean liner Queen Mary was used as a troop carrier by the British in the war. From 1940 to 1945 it carried 650,000 soldiers to various combat theatres.

(910) General Patton disengaged three divisions from combat during the Battle of the Bulge and directed them over a hundred miles on ice covered roads to relieve the American defenders of Bastogne.

(911) U-boats sunk around 3,000 ships in the war.

(912) The war for Hitler was about Lebensraum - living space for the German people. Hitler wanted Europe to essentially become one giant Germany and for the population of Germany to expand accordingly. It is ironic then that, as a result of defeat in World War 2, Germany ended up 25% smaller than it had been going into the conflict.

(913) The Allied codename for the Normandy Landings was Operation Neptune.

(914) The Germans soldiers on the western front were, on average, about five years older than the Allied soldiers. The heavy losses on the eastern front had left Germany with less young men to recruit and so the average age of the soldier was going up.

(915) The female Soviet sniper Roza Shanina had 54 confirmed kills.

(916) Coconut juice was sometimes used as an emergency substitute for blood plasma by medics in the Pacific.

(917) The Taj Mahal was covered in bamboo style scaffolding during the war to prevent it becoming a target for Japanese bombers.

(918) Night Witches was the name given to a female bomber regiment in the Soviet Union. The Night Witches dropped 3,000 tons of bombs over German lines.

(919) When it was in danger of Nazi invasion, Great Britain, just to be on the safe side, shipped its gold reserves to Canada. The gold was held in a building in Montreal. This was so top secret that most of the people who worked in the building had no idea that they were sitting on Britain's gold reserves.

(920) Only about 140 cars were built in the United States during the war. This is because all factories and industries were concentrating on the war effort.

(921) Oswald Mosley, a fascist leader who had met Hitler and Mussolini, was interned in Britain during the war. Mosley first entered the House of Commons in his early twenties and was considered to be a brilliant rising star. A charismatic speaker who looked like a film star and soon had the ear of people like Ramsay MacDonald. By his mid-thirties he was a busted flush and drifted off into fascism to be forever regarded as a dangerous and vain buffoon by most of the general public and establishment.

(922) Britain put 350,000 landmines on its beaches in preparation for a German invasion.

(923) The American Mk2 Fragmentation Grenade had a deadly 30-foot blast radius.

(924) Men from the Waffen SS Latvian Legion served as guards during the Nuremberg Trials.

(925) The British Expeditionary Force lost 50 to 60% of their artillery and tanks when they were evacuated from Dunkirk.

(926) After Dunkirk, under threat on invasion, Britain was capable of equipping about twelve army divisions with artillery. This rapidly increased though as new munitions were

produced. Infantry was less of a problem. By the middle of June 1940, Britain had 22 infantry divisions to combat a German invasion.

(927) General Omar Bradley had nearly a million men under his command in World War 2 at one point.

(928) Some German POWs who were taken to New York during the war were surprised to find the city intact. They had believed Nazi propaganda and tall tales about V-2 rockets damaging New York.

(929) During the Battle of the Bulge, German soldiers heard that General Bradley's army group had been surrounded and destroyed by a gas attack. This obviously turned out to be fake news.

(930) The Grumman F6F Hellcat was an American carrier-based fighter aircraft. The Hellcat was responsible for 56% of American air victories in the Pacific. It downed 5,163 Japanese planes at a loss of just 270 Hellcats.

(931) The Japanese defenders of Iwo Jima were deep underground in caves. The Americans had to try and blast them out and when this didn't work had to resort to hand to hand combat.

(932) Iwo Jima was not yet secure when the famous flag raising occurred but soldiers said it was a boost for morale to see the American flag flying at such a high vantage point.

(933) When the Red Army entered German soil near the end of the war they were amazed by the tidy gardens and neat well stocked houses they encountered. It made them confused as to why a country that seemed to be so rich had felt the need to invade the Soviet Union - a country where most people lived in poverty.

(934) Hitler's policy of designating towns and buildings

'Fortresses' near the end of the war didn't make any sense because the Luftwaffe was incapable of supplying the Fortresses by this point.

(935) The Siegfried Line, aka the Westwall, was a line of German fortifications built during the 1930s opposite the French Maginot Line. It stretched to around 390 miles. The Siegried Line was never really finished and although Hitler ordered it to be improved in 1944 the German generals were less than impressed with the fortifications. It didn't present an impregnable barrier to the Allies.

(936) The Maginot Line had 142 bunkers.

(937) The Maginot Line could hold half a million soldiers. It had barracks, hospitals, and hot and cold running water.

(938) The fact that the Germans could go around the Maginot Line and attack through Belgium was not something the French were unaware of. The Maginot Line was specifically designed to protect France from a frontal invasion and make the Germans launch any attack through Belgium. The French military presumed that, with the help of French and British troops, a German invasion could be defeated in Belgium. This obviously turned out to be a complete miscalculation.

(939) A lot of people in France, including an army officer named Charles de Gaulle, thought the Maginot Line was a waste of resources and that the money and material should have been spent on tanks and planes instead.

(940) After the war ended, French troops were stationed at the Maginot Line again and one of its biggest bunkers became a NATO command centre. When France left NATO, the Maginot Line was abandoned.

(941) Girls from the girls' league of the Hitler Youth were thrown into the battles near the end of the war. The Nazis were so morally bankrupt and so desperate that they were perfectly

willing to sacrifice 14 year-old girls in a futile and pointless last stand.

(942) In September of 1945, Soviet newspapers reported that Hitler was, after changing his appearance, hiding in the British occupation zone within Germany. There was no truth in these claims.

(943) Hitler's dentist confirmed that a jawbone dug up in the Reichschancellery garden did belong to Hitler.

(944) In his memoir, Field Marshal Alan Brooke said that Mountbatten (who was Supreme Allied Commander of the Southeast Asia Theatre) once came up with a scheme to use icebergs as aircraft carriers. Brooke didn't think much of this eccentric plan.

(945) The iceberg aircraft carrier scheme of Mountbatten that Brooke mentioned was clearly Project Habakkuk. Project Habakkuk was a plan by inventor Geoffrey Pike to use pykrete in the construction of floating airfields. Pykrete is a mixture of ice and wood pulp. A test ship was constructed in Canada but the project proved more time consuming and expensive than was expected so it never got off the ground.

(946) The Germans, unlike the Allies and Japanese, did not deploy aircraft carrier fleets in the war (something the Allies were grateful for). The Nazis only had one aircraft carrier (named the Graf Zeppelin which they started work on in 1936). Although the Graf Zeppelin was put to sea it was never really finished and didn't play a role in the war. The Graf Zeppelin sat in Poland for most of the war and was scuttled when the Red Army arrived.

(947) Operation Unthinkable, the plan tentatively suggested by Winston Churchill to attack the Red Army in 1945, proposed using 100,000 German soldiers to fight alongside the Allies.

(948) During the Battle for France and the Low-Countries, the Germans did attack a few sections of the Maginot Line. A few sections were destroyed but in other areas French troops managed to hold out until they learned that France had surrendered.

(949) The American M6 supertank weighed 57 tons and was supposed to be the American version of tank monsters like the Tiger. Only 40 of these tanks were ever built though.

(950) The Tank, Heavy, TOG 1 was a prototype British heavy tank produced in the early part of the war. These tanks weighed 80 tons. However, this 'super tank' never got very far off the drawing board because the British military realised they were too expensive to produce in large numbers and too heavy to be effective in the sort of mobile warfare that the conflict demanded.

(951) The Luftwaffe chiefs could have implemented jet fighter production in 1941 but at the time they expressed a preference for propeller planes. The war might have been different if Hitler had thousands of jets flying from 1941 onwards.

(952) Italy contributed about 5% of the Axis planes during the Battle of Britain.

(953) Germany's Panzer VIII, an incredible 180 tons, was the largest tank built in the war. It was named Maus (mouse). However, only one of these was ever completed.

(954) Hugo Boss supplied some uniforms for the SS and Hitler Youth during the war.

(955) The British Sten gun came about because Britain needed a reliable submachine gun that was cheap and easy to make. It only cost £2 ($10) to make a Sten. By way of comparison, it cost $200 to make an American M1A1 Thompson submachine gun.

(956) Operation Constellation was a British plan to recapture the Channel Islands in 1943. It was felt the islands would be needed as a staging post for the Allied invasion of France. Operation Constellation never went ahead in the end because the military planners felt the civilian casualties would be too high.

(957) The Heinkel He-111 could travel at 275 mph.

(958) 1.2 million tons of steel went into the Atlantic Wall.

(959) The MP 3008 was a German rip-off of the Sten gun. 10,000 of these gun were produced and a lot were given to the Volkssturm near the end of the war.

(960) In 1998, Volkswagen confirmed that it had used forced labourers during the war.

(961) The maximum speed dive of a Stuka was 373 mph.

(962) The Germans laid five million mines across the Atlantic wall.

(963) 430,000 Axis troops were involved in Operation Spring Awakening - the doomed attempt to recapture eastern European oil fields near the end of the war.

(964) Portable Germans weapons like the Panzerfaust were responsible for about 70% of Red Army tank losses in the war.

(965) Stukas flew almost 6,000 sorties in the German invasion of Poland.

(966) On August the 18th 1940, British fighter planes shot down eighteen Stukas in one day. The Stuka was slow and clumsy compared to a Spitfire or Hawker Hurricane.

(967) The Germans lost 60 Stukas in air combat in the summer of 1940.

(968) In December, 1944, 25 German POWs escaped from a prisoner of war camp in Papago Park, Arizona. They were all captured again within four weeks.

(969) It cost 3.7 billion Reichsmarks to build the French portion of the Atlantic Wall.

(970) Josef Mengele was known as the Angel of Death for the horrific experiments he performed on concentration camp victims. Sadly, Mengele managed to escape after the war. The Allies had him in custody at one point but had no idea who he really was. They didn't know he was one of the most infamous and evil Nazis. Mengele managed to get to South America and settled in Brazil. He is believed to have drowned in 1967.

(971) German prisoners of war who ended up in America often said that life in an American prisoner of war camp was much better than life in the German Army. Many put weight on because the food in the camp was better than the army rations they used to get.

(972) Portugal was officially neutral in the war but allowed the Allies to use the Azores Islands for anti-submarine purposes.

(973) An American paratrooper named Eugene Metcalfe was captured during Operation Market Garden and questioned by the SS. During this interrogation he came face to face with Heinrich Himmler. Himmler and the SS were very civil to Metcalfe and even gave him a hearty dinner of German sausages.

(974) Operation Steinbock was the name given to a German bomber offensive against Britain in the first months of 1944. It has been dubbed the Baby Blitz. The operation was designed as revenge for the Allied bombing of Germany. Hermann Göring conceived the plan as a way to destroy London and make the Allies rethink their strategy of bombing Germany. Operation Steinbock did not achieve the grandiose plans of

Göring. The Luftwaffe lost 330 aircraft in the offensive -
planes it could ill afford to lose at this stage of the war.

(975) It is speculated that as many as 25,000 children served
in military units during World War 2.

(976) Britain gave the Soviet Union 1,200 Spitfires during the
war. The Soviets had trouble with this famous plane though
because they thought that the outline of the plane was too
similar to the German BF-109s - which led to confusion for
Soviet pilots and anti-aircraft gunners.

(977) Martin James Monti was the only American officer to
switch sides in the war. The 23-year-old US Army second
lieutenant stole a plane in Italy and flew to German lines
where he asked for asylum. Monti was the son of German and
Italian parents and had fascist leanings. He was taken to
Berlin for propaganda purposes but didn't prove that much
use to the Nazis. After the war, Monti was captured by the
Americans and sentenced to 25 years in prison. He was
released in 1960.

(978) Before the atomic bombs were dropped, Japan planned
to deploy 10,000 kamikaze aircraft and 600 submarines
against the expected American invasion of their country.

(979) It is estimated that an invasion of Japan would have had
to overcome a 35 million strong force of militia and Japanese
soldiers. The Japanese were training civilians to use bombs
disguised as satchels and even schoolgirls were taught to shoot
rifles.

(980) Sweden only stopped selling ball-bearings to Nazi
Germany in 1944.

(981) A Swiss state timber company built the concentration
camp at Dachau.

(982) At the start of Operation Barborossa, the Red Army was

in a hopelessly vulnerable position. The Soviets were too far forward in defensive fortifications and were simply swallowed up in their hundreds of thousands by German pincer movements.

(983) Stalin received over eighty warnings from spies and other governments that Hitler was going to invade the Soviet Union. He still ignored these warnings though.

(984) When a politburo (the principal policymaking committee of the communist party) delegation went to visit Stalin at the start of the German invasion, Stalin initially thought they had come to arrest him.

(985) A few months into Operation Barborossa, the three German Army Groups had suffered 200,000 casualties but only received 47,000 replacements. This was an early sign of what would become a critical factor in the eastern war. Germany simply didn't have the manpower or industrial base necessary to fight a long war with the Soviet Union.

(986) Britain imported 70% of its food when war broke out. To become more self-sufficient, arable land in Britain was increased by 43% and 1.7 million more allotments were created.

(987) It took eleven months to get from D-Day to the German surrender.

(988) The United States built 88,000 landing craft in the war.

(989) General von Cholitz, the German commander of Paris, was ordered by Hitler to blow up the Eiffel Tower, the Arc de Triomphe, and Notre Dame cathedral. He was also told to destroy all the churches, monuments, and bridges in Paris. General von Cholitz, as we have noted, simply ignored Hitler's insane orders.

(990) When Hitler invaded the Soviet Union, Stalin was still

sending huge quantities of wheat and oil to Germany as part of the Nazi-Soviet Pact.

(991) When they shot the 1971 film Willy Wonka & the Chocolate Factory in Munich, the producers had to go outside of Germany to find enough dwarves to play the Oompa Loompas. There was still a shortage of dwarves in Germany because the Nazis had killed so many during the war.

(992) More Soviet planes were destroyed on the opening day of Operation Barbarossa than British planes were destroyed in the entire Battle of Britain.

(993) On the opening day of Operation Barbarossa, 25% of the Soviet Union's aircraft were destroyed out by the Germans.

(994) At the start of Operation Barbarossa, the Germans estimated that the Soviet Union could put 200 divisions into battle. In the end, the Soviet Union put 600 divisions into battle.

(995) During the Blitz, more German bombers were destroyed by accidents than by anti-aircraft guns or Allied planes.

(996) By the middle of 1944, seven million British women had been mobilised to join the war effort in auxiliary roles or the munitions industry.

(997) Eisenhower allowed a (American equipped) French Division to liberate Paris. The French Division arranged a German surrender document in Paris that made no mention of America or Britain.

(998) Swedish ships carried iron-ore to Nazi Germany for much of the war.

(999) Himmler said the goal of the campaign in the east was to reduce the 'Slavic' population by 30 million. 27 million people died in the Soviet Union so Himmler's chilling ambition was

almost met.

(1000) American shipyards launched 147 aircraft carriers in the war.